Uncommon Beginnings: A Leadership Strategy for Starting in a New Ministry

Uncommon Beginnings:
A Leadership Strategy
for Starting in a
New Ministry

by

Robert D. Kuest

New Mission Systems International

Fort Myers, Florida

Published by:

New Mission Systems International
2701 Cleveland Ave, Suite #7
Fort Myers, Florida 33901

ISBN – 978-1481864794

Cover design: Phillip Barrera, Graphics All, Fort Myers, FL

Dedication
To

Alvin F. Kuest (1916 – 1997)
and
Florence A. Kuest (1921 – 2004)

No child could ever want more loving and dedicated parents.
Their commitment to each other was exemplary.
Their dedication to Christ brought many into His Kingdom.
Their leadership brought new life and growth to their church,
a Christian camping ministry and a Christian retirement
center.
Today, they walk together in the joy of their reward in
the presence of the One they served.

UNCOMMON BEGININGS:
A Leadership Strategy for Starting in a New Ministry

TABLE OF CONTENTS

Introduction
Uncommon Beginnings:
A Leadership Strategy for Starting
in a New Ministry

What was going through Joshua's mind as he stood on the shores of the River Jordan and looked into what was called *The Promised Land*? He had to be feeling nervous about the task to which he had just been appointed. Moses was gone and now he was to be the leader. It is at this point that The Lord approaches Joshua and gives him two directives.

The first command is repeated four times. He is told to "be strong and courageous" (Jos 1:7, 9 & 18). Joshua 1:6 adds the word *very* courageous. Then, he is warned:

> Be careful to obey all the law my servant Moses gave you; do not turn from it to the right or to the left, that you may be successful wherever you go. Do not let this Book of the Law depart from your mouth; meditate on it day and night, so that you may be careful to do everything written in it. Then you will be prosperous and successful.
>
> -- Joshua 1:7-8

This book is directed to readers who have been called to be the new leader in either an existing role (as was Joshua) or a newly created situation. If you fit in this category, you are probably having some of the same thoughts that ran through Joshua's mind. The former leader is gone and now it is up to you to lead God's people into their future. As we begin a study through the leadership steps you can take to make your journey successful, my first encouragement to you would be these words given to the young man who would now lead Israel.

We also need to think about what was going through the minds of the Israelites when Joshua was presented as the new leader. Moses had been their leader for forty years. How would Joshua be different? How would he treat people? Would the goals remain the same? There are so many fears in a transitional period. From the days Joshua became the new leader of Israel, these questions in the mind of people who are receiving a new leader.

Now you find yourself as the new person; and it is possible that many of the people with whom you will work have been in the community longer than you have been alive. They have seen staff members come and go. They have outlasted the bad ones and wept as the good ones went to new ministries. They are excited about your coming, but they will hold off any evaluation of you and your ministry for a few months. They will listen patiently to your sermons, sit politely as you lead small group Bible study – but follow your leadership? That is another question and that is the purpose of this book.

Newness comes in many forms. Perhaps you are new on a mission field, or new on an existing staff, or a new volunteer leader within a congregation. The use of the words minister or ministry in this book are not to be seen as referring only to those who lead a church. The principles discussed herein will apply to any new leadership situation anywhere in the world. Whatever your situation there are many issues to be addressed. The realities of the new responsibility make beginning a traumatic time. If faced objectively, this can be a rewarding time. If they are ignored, your leadership will be nothing like you envisioned.

As a new leader you will need to make many self adjustments as you adapt your schedule, lifestyle, and thinking from your former position to this new one. The atmosphere, friendships and expectations are very different. You will need to get acquainted with new people, new expectations as you preach, teach, plan, provide services, and deal with a variety of new people and situations.

If you are married you will face major adjustments in family life. There will be new pressures and expectations put on your spouse and children. A study on church leaders and their families reports, "Among the hundreds of pastors *LEADERSHIP Journal* editors meet, interview, or correspond with each year, the specter of a marital meltdown is usually their greatest fear. No other tragedy in the ministry holds such a threat" (Merrill, *Clergy Couples*, 9). It is imperative that your decision be supported with the commitment of your spouse and that your communication skills are strong enough to see you through a life which seemingly everyone is watching.

All these issues are real and each subject could be the basis of an entire book in itself. The purpose of this book, however, is to deal with those issues directly related to *leadership strategy*, "How to be an effective leader of people from the beginning?" One study discovered that,

> Some [leaders] move into a new situation and
> do all the *right* things in the startup period. Yet
> when we questioned them about their *plan of*

ministry upon entering that situation, we discovered they had none. All the good and right things they did in their start up were done by either intuition or luck (Oswald, *Pastor as Newcomer*, 2).

This quote reveals the reason I have entitled this book *Uncommon Beginnings*. In my experience and through reading the experiences of others, the *common* leadership strategy for a new ministry is one of two: either, 1) there is no strategy, or, 2) the new leader brings a strategy from the outside. Both are destined to failure. It is my hope this book will help new leaders begin with a workable strategy that will strengthen the Kingdom of God.

If you as a new leader eel a sense of inadequacy for the task, – you are in good company. Remember Moses did not feel he was the right choice to deliver Israel (Ex 3 & 4). Gideon believed he lacked the credentials or the courage (Jdg 6). Jeremiah claimed he was too young (Jer 1:6). Amos said he was merely a shepherd and tree trimmer (Amos 7:14). Paul wondered why God chose *the chief of sinners* (1 Ti 1:15). Not one felt he was adequate; however, empowered by God's Spirit, each did mighty works. It is that same Spirit who is offered to God's servants today.

As a new leader contemplates their future there is a critical decision to make. Am I in this place to do something, or am I in this place for something to do? Or, to paraphrase leadership author Ken Blanchard, "Am I here for the sheep or are the sheep here for me?" If all you want to do is preach and teach the Word from week to week, visit the sick, marry and bury the membership (all of which are honorable services of the ministry), then there is no sense reading on. If, however, you want to lead people to accomplish something for God, perhaps these chapters can get you started.

As you begin, keep one thought in mind, leaders lead people from where they are to where they need to be. *Leadership* is an action word. You can receive training in the finest schools, take all the right classes, and not be a leader. You can have a great vision of what can be accomplished and never be a leader. You might hold an important position, such as Missionary, Apostle, Bishop, Senior Pastor, Youth Pastor, Worship Pastor, Elder, etc., but never be a leader. Leaders lead. The purpose of this book is to present a strategy for being a leader that makes a difference.

This study was born out of my feelings of being inadequately prepared to *lead* a group of people and subsequent conversations with many of my colleagues who have felt the same frustration. This is to be seen as a curriculum for preparing new ministry leaders to have a strategy for beginning an assignment has been an oversight in most ministerial colleges and seminaries. The schools do an excellent job of teaching theology, psychology, sociology and church growth. However, as I have informally interviewed ministers from a wide variety of denominational backgrounds, very few have said his/her seminary offered them a *strategy* for beginning. Research concerning leadership has found that most Protestant seminaries virtually ignore the components of a leadership strategy (Barna, *Power of a Vision*, 13).

> Many leadership courses or skills sessions teach such basic things as leading meetings and discussions, asking questions, setting up budgets, forming agendas, delegating responsibility, and organizing. These approaches are useful and necessary as

beginning points, but most programs end there. They need to go beyond that to teach the most critical things like use of intuition, developing honesty, integrity, life purpose, vision, inspiration, and wisdom... (Hagberg, *Real Power*, 169).

The first year of a ministry, whether it is stateside or foreign, is the most crucial. The first twelve to eighteen months will set the tone for the remaining years (Oswald, *Crossing the Barriers*, 7). Beginning without understanding the issues and/or having a strategy will send any leader into an emotional *meltdown* that will hit between their first and third year. Perhaps this is the reason that the average ministry lasts no more than four years (Barna, *Today's Pastors*, 36). To prevent this from happening it is imperative that the first years of leadership responsibility be positive and successful. If this strategy helps provide this sense of accomplishment, it will be well worth the effort involved.

Great Commission Leadership

The three parts of the leadership strategy presented in this book are taken from Jesus' example as He commissioned His disciples before leaving them to the work. I refer to them as *The Three Leadership Responsibilities that Cannot Be Delegated*. As Jesus spoke The Great Commission (Mt 28:19-20) he set forth His vision for how far the Kingdom of God could stretch and what it was going to take to get it there. The three tasks that cannot be delegated are:

1) Leaders must grasp the vision.
2) Leaders must influence ownership of the vision.

3) Leaders must empower others to accomplish the vision.

These functions of leadership make up the three sections into which this book is divided.

Christian leadership is a great calling, full of joy and struggle. It is my prayer that through this series of lessons new leaders will be able to find that joy and work their way through the difficulties of successfully moving God's people to where He wants them to be. If you will follow these guidelines with Christ-like integrity, you will find the joy you dreamed about when you answered God's call to lead His people.

ACKNOWLEDGEMENTS

When I set out to study for my Doctor of Ministry degree at Fuller Theological Seminary I had no idea where it was going to lead. I enjoyed the classes and with the help of the late Ray Anderson, PhD. I was able to create this curriculum designed to help Bible college graduates have a strategy for beginning their first ministry.

While writing this dissertation I prayed, "Lord, I feel privileged to be able to gain this training; I am willing to share it wherever you see it needed." At that time, teaching around the world in multi-cultural and multi-denominational settings was the furthest thought from my mind. However, with the encouragement of the leaders at First Christian Church in Anaheim, CA and men of mission experience like Ralph Brune and Phil Hudson, that prayer expanded to an international ministry.

After teaching these lessons in various mission seminars, I set out to rework the original dissertation to make it more readable to the church leaders in the countries wherein we taught. With encouragement and council from friends at New Mission Systems International – C.V. Ellott, Duane Crumb, Laura Clancy and others -- this rewrite has become a reality.

I would like to thank our friend and supporter, Ray Runkle as well as Ralph Shead of Literature and Teaching Ministry for their meticulous proof-reading. They spent untold hours going over this manuscript. Without them, this would not be presentable. And, for the third time, my thanks goes to Phil Barrera for the beautiful artwork and cover. It is only through friends like these that a book is born.

Section 1

First Leadership Responsibility

Grasping a vision

Chapter One
Understanding Vision

Introduction

As Jesus was finalizing his earthly time with his followers He gave them the task of making disciples everywhere they travelled (Mt 28:19). However, Jesus did not just give a command, he unfolded His vision of what could be accomplished – committed believers in every ethnic grouping throughout the world. His sights were not set on just a select group in the capital city. He envisioned these leaders going out from their beginnings to the people of Judea, out to Samaria, and out further to everyone on the face of the earth (Ac 1:8). There were people to recruit, there was training to be done, there were passages to book and languages to learn. All of this was predicated on a vision Jesus had given his disciples three years earlier, "Follow me and I will make you fishers of men" (Mt 4:19).

Modern Christian leaders are inspired to action by the commission Jesus gave just prior to His ascension. In His words, we can also discover that Jesus demonstrates the first responsibility in leading God's people – to motivate followers with a vision of potential. Leadership begins when a leader grasps a picture of the possibilities. Whether the people have been established for fifty years or if they are a people embarking on the beginning of a new mission, a leadership vision is an absolute necessity. Vision "is the foundation of all true leadership" (Haggai, *Lead On*, 23). It is your responsibility; you cannot delegate this task to any other person.

To be effective, a vision cannot be imported. A vision has to be built out of the present situation and shared in a way that it becomes the vision of the people. Calling for careful research and planning – this is where successful leadership begins. The temptation is to think of all the programs seen in successful organizations and allow their success to become our dream. Therefore, as the new leader, you arrive on the field with these great dreams hovering in your mind. A *vision*, however, is quite different from a dream (Malphurs, *Developing a Vision*, 30). It is possible that these dreams might become a part of your vision. The new vision, however, must be built on far more than classroom models and/or previous experience.

Because of the leadership importance of a compelling vision I want to begin by searching the biblical foundations so that you understand that this important leadership tool is not some theory derived from worldly scholarship. Next, I want to look at the leader's responsibility to be the developer and evangelist for a God-given shared vision. Then, we will close with a look at what a well articulated vision will do for your leadership.

Biblical Foundation for Vision

Jim came bursting into my office early one Monday morning and made me realize why I, as a leader, needed to understand the biblical foundation for *vision*. In my sermon the day before, I had shared my vision for the congregation. The next day, Jim, who was already unhappy with the direction the church was going, came into my office with a piece of paper in hand. He closed the door and said, "We've got to talk!" He proceeded to tell me how, after yesterday's sermon, he had gone home to look up the words, *dream* and *vision* in his dictionary. His study convinced him that my words were of the occult. He told me, "Anyone who speaks of *dreams* and *visions* must be involved in satanic rituals." Even by showing him how God had spoken through visions and how prophets had seen dreams, he was not convinced and never returned to that church.

Vision Is Biblical

Christian organizations have been criticized for borrowing leadership practices from the modern corporate world. However, the effective principles of the modern corporate world were in Scripture long before present day gurus started writing about them.

The Apostle Paul gives a clear statement of the fact that God has operated on the basis of a vision since the beginning. He writes that God had revealed His intentions to bring the entire universe together in Christ. When this happens, He will be the one Lord of all that exists" (Eph 1:9-10). God's plans are carefully revealed in visions of what can be accomplished by those who follow His leadership.

God's Vision for Israel

God shared His vision when He called Abram to become the father of many nations. He promised to bless him and keep him safe (Gen 12:1-3). As a result of his faithfulness, Abram could attempt to count the stars and try to realize how big a vision God had in mind (Gen 15:4-5). When Abram went through times when there seemed to be no fulfillment God repeated the vision as an incentive for Abram to continue. Each time He made the vision clearer

5

(Gen 17:4-8). To insure His promise God changed Abram's name to *Abraham, "father of many"* (Gen 17:5). This vision of a great nation was then passed through Abraham's generations – Isaac (Gen 22:15-18) and then Jacob (Ge 28:13-15). Even though it took four generations before it bloomed, the vision remained constant. Even today, it continues to be the anchor of hope for Israel.

After the people of promise fell into slavery, God called Moses to deliver them. From a burning bush God gave Moses a vision of Israel worshipping on the very place he was standing (Ex 3:12). Moses called the children of Israel out of Egypt with a vision of returning to the land promised to Abraham, Isaac, and Jacob (Ex 6:6-8). When Moses died, the mantle of leadership fell to Joshua. God met with Joshua and commissioned him to service by giving him a vision of a beautiful land and a promise of continued protection (Jos 1:1-9). Through Joshua this portion of God's vision was realized.

God's vision, however, went far beyond Israel. Even as He announced it to Abraham, He envisioned that all the peoples on earth would be blessed through Abraham's seed (Gen 12:3). Through Jesus, we become that seed (Gal 3:29).

Jesus' Vision for Ministry

As Jesus began His ministry He announced His vision to followers, "The Spirit of the Lord is on me . . . He has sent me to proclaim freedom for the prisoners and recovery of sight for the blind, to set the oppressed free, to proclaim the year of the Lord's favor," (Lk 4:18-19). Having fulfilled the Messianic vision of the prophets, Jesus told them that His Father's original vision of blessing the nations was still in process, "When the Son of Man comes in His glory, and all the angels with him. . . all the nations will be gathered before Him" and there will be a judgment (Mt 25:31-33).

> Jesus stands all by himself as *the* transformational leader. He was able to create, articulate and communicate a compelling vision; to change what people talk about and dream of; to make his followers transcend self-interest; to enable us to see ourselves and our world in a new way; to provide prophetic insight into the very heart of things; and to bring about the highest order of change (Ford, *Transforming Leadership*, 106).

Christian leaders should never be ashamed to talk in the terms of *vision*. It is a tool God has constantly used in leading His people. It remains a powerful and valid tool for leading His people. But who is responsible for grasping this vision?

Vision Is a Leader's Responsibility

When I graduated from college I had a huge dream. There was a world out there to impact. I felt that with the skills I had gained in school, I was going to be able to make great strides for the Kingdom. I could not wait to begin. As I drove across the country to my first pastorate, all the dreams were mine. They had nothing to do with the people in the village who were about to receive me as their new pastor – another face in an eighty year history. I believed they would surely capture my dream. However, I soon learned that my dream had little to do with their situation.

Leadership author Aubrey Malphurs writes,

Vision is crucial to any ministry. Ministry without vision is like a surgeon without a scalpel, a cowboy who has lost his horse, a carpenter with a broken hammer. To attempt a ministry without a clear, well-articulated vision is to invite a stillbirth (Malphurs, *Developing a Vision*, 17).

The misunderstanding of *vision* is the first seed of discouragement and burnout for many leaders in a new ministry. To prevent this from happening to you, it is best to begin your new assignment with leadership knowledge intact, ready to draw upon it to meet the needs of people, rather than fulfill dreams you brought with you. Then, upon arrival, carefully work with the people so that any vision becomes their vision, conformed to specific needs. Many new leaders, however, along with others who have yet to learn through their struggles, will try to force his/her vision (one usually formed away from the present locality) on people who have no understanding or ownership of it.

It is true; it is a leader's responsibility to dream the dream that can become reality.

Someone . . . must paint the dream. For anything to happen there must be a dream. And for anything great to happen there must be a great dream. The growing edge [leader] will be a painter of great dreams for *all* of its people, something to lift their sights above the ordinary and give them a great goal to strive for – something for each person to strive for (Greenleaf, *Servant Leadership*, 88).

As mentioned earlier, this is one of the three leadership tasks that you cannot delegate to someone else. Other people may be involved, but you, as the leader, are the *point person* - the central figure in the process of getting others to see solutions for meeting needs that others have not seen or could not believe to be possible.

The power of a leader with vision is illustrated by my friends Rutherford and Tsahai Banda in the African nation of Malawi. Rutherford was born and raised in a small village on the Lilongwe Plain. He knows the land and the people. He and his wife have a passion for planting village churches, leadership training and orphan care. God gave them a small piece of land and a vision for an orphan facility which would provide housing, training and protection to young girls in abusive environments.

On a recent visit we made to Malawi Rutherford said, "Let me show you something." We walked out on a level piece of property covered only with grass and dead trees. As we look at that emptiness, Rutherford began to describe a two-story building with dorm rooms, classrooms and an adjoining house where the matrons would live.

Where others had looked and saw grass and trees, Rutherford saw God's potential. He helped me see the size of the rooms, the height of the adobe block building. With his help I could see young girls living and working, laughing and playing. He helped me to see what he was seeing.

An architect once told me, "A building is built three times. First, it is created in the mind of the designer. Second, it is drawn on paper. Then, finally, it is actually constructed."

What I am talking about in this lesson is that first *seeing* that begins the road to accomplishment. This is the power of a vision. Your ability to see needs and solutions that others are not seeing.

The Purpose of a Vision

Vision Leads People

There are two problems that thwart many visions. The first we have already mentioned – bringing a vision in from an outside source. A second problem you may face is that your vision is limited to the expectation of the people around you. You may be leading people who have fallen into a rut after years of tradition and discouragement. Leadership, however, is what "enables an organization to bridge the chasm between where it is and where it should be" (Smith, *Learning to Lead,* 21). Through careful encouragement you can help the people to believe that there can be a future greater than today. (We will discuss what can be done in sections two and three).

Vision Gives Hope

During a seminar workshop on *Writing a Purpose Statement for Your Church*, I asked the participants to share why they were in the workshop. One pastor from a Middle American community raised his hand, "I really don't know why I came to this session; my church will be dead in five years." I asked him why he was so sure. "It is a downtown church, next to the river." he replied, "All the members are moving out. I have been hired to give it a decent burial." I said, "You can change that simply by giving a vision of a different picture of the next five years." "No," he answered, "It is going to die."

It is possible that this pastor of the dying church would have had a tough time selling a vision of new life. Nevertheless, he and the people had already given in to a image for their future. Many dying organizations could be reborn if only someone would challenge them to a new vision and promise to stay and help them achieve it.

A vision of the future not only keeps hope alive, it also becomes the stabilizer through troubled times. Because vision is a "picture held in your mind's eye of the way things could or should be" (Barna, *Power of Vision,* 29) it acts as the beacon light that leads a ship through troubled water.

There was a time when the church where I served was navigating in stormy waters. I consulted a pastor friend as to what he would suggest I could do to bring the people through to calmer seas. He asked me, "Do you have a vision for what the church can be?" When I affirmed that I did, he asked, "Have they heard it and accepted it?" "Probably not in the past year," I reflected. "Then get up in front of your people," he said, "and announce it again, loud and clear."

I followed my friend's advice. My sermon the next Sunday morning was "I Have a Dream!" That same evening I shared "How We Can Reach the Dream Together". That happened to be the Sunday of the regular Board Meeting and, with the Chairman's permission I shared a third time on "What We, As Leaders, Can Do to Bring the Dream." I was amazed at what these restatements of vision did for the people. They refocused on what we were trying to do. The congregation saw the future greater than the present problems and moved ahead with determination. Within a month, we had moved beyond the problem that had stifled us for nearly six months.

In his book, *The Purpose-Driven Church*, Rick Warren relates *The Nehemiah Principle*. "Vision and purpose must be restated every twenty-six days to keep the church moving in the right direction" (Warren, *Purpose-Driven Church*, 111).

A vision is "our window on the world of tomorrow" (Kouzes and Posner, *Leadership Challenge*, 89). It provides hope to people that they can accomplish something for the Lord. It is breath of life that is needed in so many Christian organizations. At a meeting with several church leaders, I asked, "How many of you have a vision of what your ministry can be?" Less than half raised their hand. It is no wonder that congregations are stagnated. If leaders have no hope in the future, neither will the people.

Vision Gives a Foundation for Planning

When you grasp a vision and communicate it orally and in writing, it creates a future. However, the process that leads to a shared vision is not easy. One famous business leader said, "Visionaries are constantly fighting conventional wisdom because they see the world ahead in terms of what it can be if someone is willing to look at things in very different ways" (John Scully, quoted in Kouzes and Posner, *Leadership Challenge*, 66). Many leaders will have forgotten how to look beyond the present; some will only look at the past.

The vision to which leaders direct their people is based upon a study of the present situation. Later I will share some exercises that will help you think creatively for a vision particular to your present situation.

> If there is a spark of genius in the leadership function at all, it must lie in this transcending ability, and kind of magic, to assemble – out of a variety of images, signals, forecasts and alternatives – a clearly articulated vision of the future that is at once simple, easily understood, clearly desirable, and energizing (Bennis & Nanus, *Leaders,* 103).

When this vision is understood, it will become the foundation and guide for all planning. Every building project has to begin with a foundation, else it collapses. The same is true for Christian organizations. As much as it sounds like heresy, "the Bible is not enough." The vision gives a foundation for planning how the Bible message will best be spread throughout your community. "Vision is the center-piece of strategy; strategy is the means to effective church development; effective development of the church is the means to transforming the world with His love" (Barna, *The Power of Vision,* 135).

Vision Gives Direction

Children love to play with balloons. They hug them and bounce them and create fun games. A favorite involves blowing into the balloon and then releasing it. The escaping air causes the balloon to fly back and forth, up and down all around the room. It is fun to watch. However, there is little fun in watching a Christian organization with no shared vision bouncing around like a balloon with no clear purpose. The writer of Proverbs describes a people without a vision as a stampede of animals (Pr 29:18 Hebrew translation).

Not only will a shared vision give people hope and a foundation, it will keep them from wandering. A vision helps your people know where they are going, why they are going there, and how to get there. Too many organizations wander aimlessly from week to week. Their leadership only exists to check on the hired help and vote on repairs to the building. There is no sense of purpose other than the doors have to be open next week and the people need to be fairly comfortable. Such thinking does not require great leadership; it only requires maintenance. And as one author put it, the problem with maintenance leadership is that leaders get so "caught up in patching leaks that (they) don't see that the ship is headed for an iceberg" (LePeau, *Paths of Leadership*, 108).

There is no easy way to go into the future. It is a rocky road at best, and only those dedicated to a vision of what can become will make a difference. These are the people willing to become pioneers into unmapped terrain, who can look at a grassed field with dead trees and see a facility dedicated to care for abused girls. In this sense the vision acts as a compass. Without it, an organization can easily lose direction and find itself lost in the desert of despair. Vision keeps us on course and leads to accomplishment.

Vision Gives a Call for Action

Seeing the future unfold with purpose leads to new life and commitment among the people, even people such as those mentioned in the inner city church located next to the river. A vision will mobilize resources – time, money, knowledge, space and especially people. A fresh new future is a strong motivation.

An effective vision is set in the future to become a beacon light to draw people to the goal. As a destination marked on a map, it will also provide a sense of comfort as people will know they are on course. They can picture where they are headed and what it will be like when they arrive. If people do not know where they are headed it is impossible to know what is needed to accomplish it, let alone know when they have arrived. A good leader provides a picture of the destination and what will be needed to get there.

Vision Gives a Sense of Individuality

An effective vision will also show why this ministry is different than any other. The vision will challenge followers and attract new members.

Nearly every church wants to "win this city to Christ." Look through the ads in the Religious Section of an American newspaper. Listed there are statements of vision and what each church believes will attract people to their door. You will notice the repetition of phrases like, *Bible Centered, Family Oriented,* and *Outstanding Music.* There are short statements declaring what sets them apart from others. What you *do not* find on this page might be the spark that sets your vision. Before striking out on a quest to write an ad, do your homework. You need to know the community. Understand their past. Dissect neighborhoods. Take the time to build a solid, shared vision that meets needs. Then communicate it to the people and help them experience the joy of fulfilling it.

The "Stump Speech"

A *stump speech* refers to political campaigns in early American history. Before public address systems, politicians would gather people around them to hear their talk. They would stand on a tree stump in order to be seen as they delivered their message telling people why they should vote for them. Because of the location and situation, the speech would have to be very short and to the point. This became known in political campaigning as a *stump speech*. You can use the same idea to tell people about the vision.

As mentioned earlier, it is your responsibility to establish the vision. It is also your task to communicate it and gain its ownership. One Christian research specialist reports that many Christian organizations in the United States suffer from an absence of leadership vision. He writes, "How frustrating to find a church that is anxious to follow its leader but has no idea in what direction it is being led" (Barna, *Power of Vision*, 142). People with a clear sense of direction are a motivated community that can only get stronger. This is not only true for churches; it identifies a problem facing all Christian organizations.

When the vision is clear in the mind of your leaders, develop it into a three-minute *Stump Speech* that can be delivered whenever and wherever you are given an opportunity (Peters, *Thriving on Chaos*, 406). Work it into team meetings, sermons, prayers, fellowship times, and conversations. You must know it well enough to have it condensed; say it simply, boldly, and often.

Now that you understand the need to develop a shared vision with your people, we need to answer the question, "How does a leader *grasp* a vision?" Let me share some principles I have found that can help.

Listen for a Vision

The art of listening might seem a strange subject at this point in a study of leadership. Listening, however, is very critical to all that is discussed throughout this book. It is the key to hearing God's agenda. It is also a means to grasping a vision that is individual to a particular situation.

Vision comes through reading, talking, observing, and asking – all of which are listening exercises. You need to build the vision by learning to hear what is being said. Without the ability to listen you will fail. If you desire to successfully share a vision, let me suggest six listening skills that will help you understand the proper vision for your people.

Listen for God's Agenda

In a class at Fuller Theological Seminary I heard a young pastor talk about his frustration with getting people to accept his vision. He threw his hands up and asked, "What can I do?" Behind him a student asked a question that caused an uneasy silence throughout the room, "Are you sure you are trying to get them to own your agenda, or God's?" The young pastor was experiencing what Barna's research uncovered, "If you are not truly seeking to build His Kingdom but to build something or somebody else's, you probably will fail and will have to regroup" (Barna, *Power of*

17

Vision, 74). The young man who asked the first question began to weep and admitted that he had never prayed for God's vision, nor had he asked for input from his leadership.

The vision of leadership must flow from above. It is a product of God working in us. God creates the vision and we receive it. Vision will arise out of your burden to know the will of God and to call people to it, to become whatever it is God wants you and His church to become. It was Nehemiah's quest to rebuild the city because God had put in his heart what to do for Jerusalem (Neh 2:12). Our constant prayer should be, "God, help me to become what You meant for me to become when You designed me; and do the same for these people I lead."

If the vision is solely yours, it will be your energies that will be expended, and you will be discouraged because there will be little blessing. The people receiving the vision will seem apprehensive; and will do little to inaugurate the new direction. Many leaders fighting this condition are ultimately discouraged and bitter. Instead of looking at their leadership tactics, they blame "those people who don't want to accomplish anything for God."

It is common for leaders to complain about the lack of initiative for God among their people; however, sometimes the opposite is true. There are many *followers* who desire to move forward but find no vision [from their leader]" (Fullum, *The View from Above*, 16). Pray fervently for God's vision, listen for it and lead the people to accomplish it.

Listening with Your Ears

Desiring to be effective, you must tune your ears to what the people are saying. This has been called "The Art of Listening." Without this skill you will become either a frustrated *lone ranger* or a *military dictator*. Consultant Myron Rush believes every person in a leadership capacity feels that they either represent a larger group of people or a *cause*. Because of this, there is an innate need to be heard. If this need *to represent* is ignored, you will become embroiled in conflict. The people must sense your willingness to hear them; willingness to accept their ideas and feelings. Knowing that, it is from this point you guide your people to where they need to be. This does not mean there will always be agreement, but the people will appreciate that they are allowed to voice their opinions and questions.

The Awesome Power of the Listening Ear (Drakeford) should be required reading for every person aspiring to lead others. The author begins, "Of all the tasks you have ever undertaken, this will be the most frustrating, annoying, and aggravating if you are not altogether sold on its significance" (Drakeford, *The Awesome Power of the Listening Ear*, 11). There is a big difference, he writes, between *hearing* and *listening*.

> *Hearing* is a word used to describe the physiological sensory processes by which auditory impressions are received by the ears and transmitted to the brain. *Listening,* on the other hand, refers to a more complex psychological procedure involving interpreting

and understanding the significance of the sensory experience (Drakeford, 17).

I missed this early in my ministry when a man came to me to explain how some of the people felt. My response was, "I'm the one with the education and you called me to lead. When it comes to leading this church, I am the expert." How wrong I was! I could have saved myself a lot of leadership grief had I listened to what the people felt.

Listening is a skill that is often overlooked because of our pride. Willingness to listen does not constitute agreement with what is heard, but it does mean that the people have been given a chance to share their hopes, needs, cares and fears. However, the ears are only one God-given organ for listening. There are two.

Listening with Your Eyes

Most people have heard the expression, "What you are doing speaks so loudly that I cannot hear what you are saying." Body language and facial expressions are so much a part of the communication process that those who refuse to *listen* to them can have their leadership stymied.

I remember sitting in a popular small town restaurant seeking a man's professional input on a very important issue I was facing. All the time I was talking, he was looking around to see who he knew. I was pouring out my heart and he was greeting nearly everyone who walked through the door. I felt that if I had gotten up and walked out, he would have never noticed. A week later he called me to ask how I was doing; however, he had all the facts mixed up. Even though his body was present, he did not understand anything I was sharing. I never again sought that man's counsel.

In teaching sessions on *Communication* we invite eight people to participate in a "skills session." We pair them up and have each pair face one another. However, before they sit down, each group is privately instructed. One group is told to think of a life-story that was very meaningful to them and plan to share it with their partner. The second group receives individual instructions. One is told to look around the room, another is told to read a book/paper while their partner is sharing. A third is told to "get caught up in" the story of the person next to them (rather than their partner across from them). The fourth person is told to keep looking at their watch and glancing at the door/window as their partner is sharing. It only takes a couple of minutes to see the person sharing their story begin to become very agitated.

What plays out in a controlled situation often causes deep problems in reality. To listen with your eyes simply means to look at the person who is speaking and use facial expression to show that you are tuned in. That sounds easy, but notice how often you talk to people who never look at you. Few experiences are more frustrating than to try to talk to a person who is constantly looking somewhere else. Eye contact helps the person sharing the ideas and feelings to know you are truly interested in them.

Listening for the Real Message

A fourth important skill in listening is to hear the message behind the words. Does the tone of voice or use of vocabulary tell a different message than the perceived words? Communication experts warn about a *hidden agenda*

–the true message behind the words. If you miss this, the significance of the words will be missed. For instance, the person who says, "Several people think. . ." is most likely sharing their own opinion. The wise preacher who authored the Proverbs cautions against the person "who winks with his eye, signals with his feet and motions with his fingers" (Pr 6:13). This might not always be true, but it does underscore the need to listen for the real message.

The Listening Reply

The fifth skill for listening to build and share a vision is the ability to ask short clarifying questions that keep the conversation on track and encourage the speaker to continue sharing. When they have finished revealing their hopes, needs, cares and fears, they feel they have been heard and are more willing to grant the leader permission to pursue the vision. Also, as the leader, you will better understand what is needed to influence a shared vision. However, questions are only one way to engage the sharer to this point.

> The effective listener must learn the skill of a reply which indicates he is intensely interested in all that is being said. A second and equally important function of the reply is as a pump primer aimed at stimulating and facilitating the flow of speech and the expression of feelings and ideas (Drakeford, *The Awesome Power,* 58).

A reply to the one sharing will show them that you have cared enough to really hear what they have shared. It might be a short summary, "What I hear you saying is..." or further inquiry, "Can you expand on what you mean by...?" In either direction, the person feels validated and what they are sharing is important.

The questions and replies will also help the conversation stay on track. In case of an interruption the listener can return and say, "You were telling me . . ." This will help the person's confidence and promote the opportunity to share the vision with them.

Conclusion

There can be no vision that belongs to the people that has not grown out of hours of listening. "Successful leaders...are *great askers*, and they do pay attention" (Bennis & Nanus, *Leaders*, 96). A vision for the future is one of the most important ingredients of any leadership recipe. Without it there simply is no credible leadership, and the door is open to dictatorship, mediocrity, or death.

The development of a vision is a strong biblical principle of leadership. God works toward a vision of having a people for Himself. Jesus worked toward a vision of His message spreading to every nation. We, too, must grasp a vision that compliments theirs and work towards its fulfillment.

If you desire to be a successful Christian leader, you *must* spend time listening to your people. You *must* ask the right questions to build the direction. Do not be caught in the temptation to take short-cuts. Most of all, communicate the vision in such a way that your people will call the vision *theirs*.

Chapter Two
Understanding Organizational Culture

Introduction

The content of this chapter presents one of the single most common reasons for leadership failure within the first year of a new assignment. And yet, many leaders and leadership students believe they do not have the time to invest in this study; therefore, they forge ahead clueless of the storm on the horizon. When it hits, it is always someone else's fault.

I was raised in central California where I became a Christian at the age of ten. After high school I attended a college in Southern California and served as a youth minister for three years. When I decided to go to seminary I chose one in the mid-west. While in seminary I was called by a small rural church to be its pastor. I survived those first years because I expected this village congregation to function differently. However, after graduation from seminary, I received my baptism by a fire ignited by my false assumptions and my inability to understand the culture in this larger community.

Because both the church and the town were bigger than my previous charge, I expected to be able to lead the same way and have similar visions as I had experienced in larger California congregations. My vision did not fit the culture. I did not survive. I hope this chapter will help to spare others the pain caused by neglecting to understand the culture of the church and its community before beginning to make changes.

25

Nervousness is an understandable reality as one begins any new responsibility; but, for many, it seems to only add to the fire inside them to make a difference. You bring to your new assignment a vision of possibilities. You are energized to create a specific vision. You are aware of the words of wise King Solomon who noted that "where there is no vision [NIV – *revelation*], the people run astray" (Pr 29:18). As a shepherd searches for green pastures, a leader constantly searches for ways to serve the needs of people while keeping them headed in God's intended direction.

Max DePree, a Christian who was very successful corporate leader, claims that your first responsibility as a leader is to *define reality* (DePree, *Leadership Is an Art*, 9). The first step in understanding your current situation is to learn the inner-workings of the organization – what makes it function the way it does? To effectively present a vision and bring about God's agenda for the people, it is important to learn to assess the current conditions and the "way things are done here." To do this, you must uncover a very powerful dynamic force that resides within any organization – its culture.

People often think of culture as being the beliefs and rituals of a foreign nation. Missionaries have long studied cross-cultural dynamics. However, every group you serve will require some cross-cultural understanding. Each one will have its unique culture. To attempt to work within any leadership situation without gaining cultural understanding will be as devastating as a missionary going to a foreign field and attempting to implement his/her thinking without attention to local culture. The study of organizational culture, therefore, is a necessary prerequisite to being able to formulate and implement any strategies for carrying out your mission.

Culture Defined

Culture begins when "A number of people *share* a common view of a problem and develop a *shared* solution" (Schein, *Organizational Culture*, 149). As any organization is given birth it begins with a purpose - to be a church, a hospital, a college, etc. As this purpose is fulfilled, many decisions have to be made, directions set, crises overcome, people hired, fired, promoted, and demoted. From these events, a set of values rises to the surface that begins to control the thinking of the entire organization; that thinking is its *culture*. You will discover the components of this environment as you begin to understand the symbols, ideologies, language, beliefs, rituals, and myths that define it. Even though the components of culture may not always be visible, they still remain the life blood of how the organization is managed and decisions are made. Culture is,

> The deeper level of *basic assumptions* and *beliefs* that are shared by members of an organization, that operate unconsciously, and that define in a basic 'taken-for-granted' fashion an organization's view of itself and its environment" Schein, *Organizational Culture*, 4).

Strong Christian leadership is not built overnight. It grows and evolves over a long period of time until consistencies are felt and assimilated in the thinking and actions of the community (even inconsistencies become consistent and

27

form their part of the culture). *Culture* is the outcome of how people view and feel about how these situations were handled.

Eventually, culture will control the success or failure of the organization. Therefore, it becomes imperative that leaders coming into a new situation study and understand that culture. Your job as a leader is to recognize and begin to manage this system of shared values. And, as God directs, you are to introduce and manage necessary change. "The only thing of real importance that leaders do is to create and manage culture" (Schein, *Organizational Culture*, 2).

The Evolution of Culture

As you experience and observe the values held by the people. The first place to begin is to uncover the motives and the character of the founder(s). This will be true even in an older organizations where the founders have long ago passed away. The values of those who laid the foundation can remain long after their departure.

As the organization grows and more people are brought in, the values of the founders begin to be accepted as the norm for new members. The stories about how the leadership handled different problems or survived difficult situations, how it began a new program, or how it dealt with a discipline situation, become the demonstration of the particular culture. These actions, along with their ensuing stories, reinforce the group's picture of itself and, thus, the culture becomes more ingrained. It begins to define them: growing, dying, serving, or demanding.

I discovered the power of culture when I accepted a call to a church in Arizona. The congregation had been birthed six years earlier by a pastor with a strong magnetic personality. When he left, the leadership called a fine man of opposite personality. The first man was charismatic and unstructured. Under his leadership, the people proudly wore the tag, *The Maverick Church* – "we don't do things the way most churches do." The second man was very scholarly and proper. Everything was to be done according to the book. The first man was seldom seen dressed in a suit; the second was never seen (even at church picnics) without a black suit.

After a few months, under the leadership of the second man, the church declined, nearly closing its doors; and the new pastor was blamed. (The leaders would not accept partial responsibility for the decline due to the fact that prior to the new man coming, the congregation relocated to a facility too small for the present attendance). Some of the people who were uncomfortable with the new man's personality soon left. Other unhappy people began a movement to rid the church of this threat to their picture of themselves. The end result was the dismissal of the second minister – not because of his incompetence, but because he did not fit the *culture*.

I was called to follow the dismissed pastor. By God's grace I lasted seventeen years and became the *culture setter*, creating the environment for the man who followed me.

The Power of Culture
In Decision Making

My second ministry was in a larger Midwest church. I was impressed with the way the leaders were organized. Everything was carefully spelled out in by-laws and seemed to be followed with precision. However, I soon noticed that what was decided within meetings was not always what actually took place. Somehow, somewhere, decisions were being altered. It took me months to discover the decision-making culture. I will share my discovery later in this chapter.

All major, and most minor, decisions within an organization will be influenced by the underlying culture. The tougher and more widespread the impact of the decision, the more the true culture will arise. In the face of a difficult decision dynamics never seen in the normal operations will begin to take hold and control the actions of the people. If you enter a new responsibility and try to make changes without understanding how decisions are truly made, you might be in for a short stay.

A problem faced by ministries arises when a powerful, popular leader – especially a founder – leaves or dies. Immediately, the organization is thrown into a *power vacuum*. Because the people have depended upon this individual's thinking and strength for so long, they no longer remember how to make decisions on their own. This will cause a period of floundering until new leadership is established to carry the cultural banner – or has earned the right to create another. Beware, however, of a possible group waiting in the wings for the *culture maker* to be out of the picture. They will try to use the power vacuum to establish their agenda. A new leader is likely to be caught in the middle of the ensuing conflict and take the blame for it.

In Adding to the Fellowship

A man came to me after his first visit and said, "I like your church. I was a deacon in the church back home, how do I become a leader here?" I told him that we only considered people for leadership after they had attended for a year. (We had experienced some major problems that led to this decision and culture is created by shared solutions to problems.) The man replied, "I cannot wait that long." He never returned.

I have had people choose to not return because they were uncomfortable with people raising their hands in worship, or having drums, or the way we participated in the Lord's Supper. I have also seen members of the congregation shun visitors who seemingly did not fit in — ethnicity, clothing, etc. I have had several occasions where a person has said, "God has sent me here to change this congregation." However, after a while they leave because they were not able to break the culture. If you enter your new calling with this mindset, you will probably be leaving after a short period of deep frustration because those who have adopted this culture will block your attempts to bring changes without earning the right to do so.

Many organizations are marked by cultures so strong that a new person either buys into their norms or leaves. Before accepting a responsibility you must ask yourself, "Can I thrive and succeed in this culture?" If you believe this is where God has called you, then make the long-term commitment to attempt change.

Culture is an unwritten qualifier of acceptability. Newcomers comfortable within the established culture (which includes doctrinal tenets) feel free to join; while those who disagree with it, and are unable to change it, find they must leave. This leaving can be the source of conflict or split if those leaving have gathered a following to their agenda.

Subcultures

An added dimension to cultural study is that of *subcultures*. Not only does every organization have an established culture, but every committee, fellowship group, and clique within the ministry will have its own shared culture that sets this unwritten criteria to who can be added. They will also have decision-making realities, as well as all other cultural criteria. It is very possible that these will be different from those of the established greater culture. Therefore, the study of the culture will never end.

If you will take the time to understand the formation and working of culture, you will be able to lead with more effectiveness. The study of how the culture was formed, however, is only the beginning. Having assessed the underlying agenda of your assignment, we need to move on to the study – or the establishment of – its mission and its values; both are pre-requisites to solid strategic planning for vision fulfillment. Again, to overlook this important area of organizational culture can lead to frustration and discouragement.

Culture Discovered

When I accepted the call to an older established church (during my second year they celebrated their centennial), I had completed my doctoral studies and had written this chapter for my dissertation. I decided to "practice what I preach." Before coming to this church I was warned about a certain couple who had caused the two former pastors much grief (both men had been terminated after short ministries). I took the questions that I had adapted from Schein's study on organizational culture and visited each leader in their home, beginning with the couple of which I had been warned. They were more than happy to share the church's history and the "way-things-are." Following that meeting in their home and for the next six and a half years, this couple was one of my greatest supporters and encouragers, even as we made significant cultural changes.

The following section is an outline of the questions to help uncover culture.[1] This is not a questionnaire to be passed out among people. This is not a list of questions for an interview. The answers to these questions should be recorded in private after you listen and observe. Plan to visit a cross section of people in their homes, or in small groups. Let them share their history. Listen with a trained ear and discover some of the answers to the questions. A noted leadership author writes:

> The leader who leads must understand the culture, which comes from reading, listening, visiting, and observing. The leader learns to understand people by going where they work, visiting in their homes, sharing their joys and

sorrows, and sticking close enough that leadership is not divorced from followership (Anderson, *Dying for Change*, 190).

Do not be surprised, or discouraged, if it takes a year or more to discover this information. Speed is *not* the goal. *Understanding* is the goal – in-depth insight that will help a leader build and share a vision. Your tenure of service might depend on how thoroughly you do your research. Edgar Schein is one of the world's foremost authorities on organizational culture. He observes,

> I have not found a reliable, quick way to identify cultural assumptions. Sometimes such assumptions are obvious at the outset; sometimes they are highly elusive, even after months of study; and sometimes one must conclude that there are no shared assumptions working across the organization because of a lack of shared history (Schein, *Organizational Culture*, 135).

With this in mind as you visit your people, listen for the answers to the following questions.

Questions about Organizational History

The best way to come to an understanding of a culture[2] is to return to its beginnings. Even organizations that have passed into the second and third generation have a culture that is rooted in its original purposes. Uncover the founding dream and any remnants of that original dream which continues to shape life and ministry. Every organization (and every person within it) has their own unique *story*. There is a real joy in listening and learning what they are.

To uncover the organization's *story*, listen for these clues:

1. Why does this church/mission/organization exist? What is its core mission?

2. Which people group have they attempted to reach?

    a. Is it basically a biological group reaching only to its families?
    b. Is there a real concern to reach beyond its own family groups to new comers?
    c. What is their cultural heritage?
    d. What is the economic status?
    e. Is either of these (cultural or economical factors) changing in the demographic area? If so, is there a desire to change?

3. What do you know about the organization's history?

    a. Why was it founded here?
    b. What major crises has it been through?
    c. Has it gone through any crucial transitions – "*watershed issues, turning points* that influenced the shape and priorities of today's congregation" (Schaller, *Looking in the Mirror*, 90)?
    d. What themes have been followed in these transitions?
    e. When were the "best days" in its history?

4. How were the crises situations handled?

    a. Look for consistencies in the actions of individuals and groups.

    b. Look for phrases that are keys to culture:
* "It has *always* been done this way" = tradition.
* "This is the *right* way to do it" = religious/moral dogma.
* "This is the way (a person or group) wanted it" = strong leader or leadership group.
* "It was debated and resolved in committee and the board" = conflict/debate.
* "It came out of our study" = openness.

Questions about Time Orientation

It will be important to discover whether the thinking of the people is planted in the past or headed for the future.

1. As people talk about the organization's present needs, what is their time focus?

    a. "We used to..." "We were..." = Orientation toward the past.

    b. "We are..." "We have been..." = Orientation toward the present.

    c. "We are going to..." = Orientation toward the future.

2. What is the determining factor in major decisions?

    a. What was?

b. What is?
c. What will be?

3. Is time an important element to most leaders?

  a. Projects are required to be accomplished on time?
  b. Projects are completed close to scheduled time?
  c. Project deadlines are put off again and again?

Questions about Space Priorities

In my first pastorate a small Sunday school class of adults met in the largest and nicest room. In the meantime, a high school class of fifteen students was stuffed into the smallest room. It was a clear insight into the culture of the congregation.

Who gets what space and what amount in the buildings will be a clue as to which group is most important to the people. Cultural consultant Schein writes:

> Organizations develop different norms of who should have how much and what kind of space. In most organizations the best views and locations are reserved for the highest-status people. Some organizations use space allocation as a direct status symbol.
> Where things are located, how they are built, the kind of architecture involved, the decorations encouraged or allowed, the furnishings – all the things that provide the visual environment – will vary from one

organization to the next and may well reflect deeper values and assumptions held in the larger culture and by the key leaders (Schein, *Organizational Culture*, 98).

Do not try to change these space priorities until you have a thorough understanding of the cultural reasons and have earned the right to suggest changes.

1. Which groups have the largest space?
2. Which rooms are maintained the best?
3. Which rooms have the best furnishings?
4. Is there any consistency in the above answers to show a pattern of value?

Questions about Leaders and Workers

Train your ear to listen for often repeated stories known as *campfire stories*. These tales reveal the key people and events which have shaped organizational culture. They will be repeated again and again to develop a firm explanation for *the way things are*. These stories shaped the value system.

1. Who are the *heroes* and *villains* of their history?

a. What is being said about them?
b. What does this tell about spoken and unspoken values?
c. Are there cases where some people call a *villain* a *hero* or vice versa?

2. How are people recruited into leadership?

    a. What is the selection process?
    b. Who really has the final say about new leaders? (In many churches names put into nomination are never considered. Who makes that determination? Why?)
    c. Are leaders selected through popularity, qualification, or to fill a quota?

3. How are workers recruited?

    a. Are they "Warm bodies to fill a need?"
    b. Are they the result of training and qualification?
    c. "Everyone is expected to do their part?"

4. How are new staff members chosen?

    a. Was there a *Search Committee*? If so, who were its constituents?
    b. Did the selectors have the final say, or did they only make recommendation to another group of leaders?
    c. Are there key individuals or groups to whom leaders "must be introduced"?
    d. Was there a group of people who enthusiastically came to you as the new leader trying to give their input on what needs to be done?

5. Is there any system for accountability for leaders and workers?

a. Is leadership a ministry to fulfill or a vote to be cast?
b. Are people put into leadership hoping that the organization will gain advantage?
   1) "Maybe they'll start attending more regularly."
   2) "He is a strong financial supporter."
   3) "She is a business leader in the community."

6. Is there any provision for rewards to those who faithfully serve, or is service taken for granted?

Questions about How Problems Are Solved

As you listen, try to identify problems that the group faced from "outside forces" (city codes, neighbor resistance, injury lawsuit, etc.). Trace the solution that was brought to these problems to gain an understanding as to what steps will be taken for similar problems in the future problems

1. How was the problem approached?

   a. *Proactive Orientation*: act to solve problems, nothing is impossible, fight, win, try.
   b. *Reactive Orientation*: accept fate, relax and enjoy what is inevitable.

2. Are there definable groups within the organization who feel they would have handled situations better?

3. How was one approach chosen over the other?

Questions about the Power Center

Often the *power center* of an organization is not found in the selected leaders. Earlier in this chapter I promised to share how I discovered the *power-center* of the church that looked to be so well structured. After every Elders' Meeting (which took place the first Sunday of the month following evening worship) I was invited by a group of men to join them for pie and coffee at a local restaurant. For several months I declined because I needed to be home with my young family. One evening about six or eight months into my ministry I accepted their invitation. I discovered that the major decisions for the church were not made in the Elders' meetings; they were made over pie and coffee. Decisions were either changed or ignored by this group of five or six men. I learned that if I wanted to introduce something new to the leadership, it had to be done over pie and coffee.

It is important to find, and work with, the true *power center* to bring about change within the organization. Ignoring the *power center* will lead to disappointment.

> As a person new to the [church], you may speculate as to who these power people are. Some of your [people] will no doubt attempt to inform you on these matters... [it is possible that] the way decisions get made in the [church] either confuses or dumbfounds you. When this happens, more than likely those in decision-making positions are checking with some other people on the sidelines (Oswald, *New Beginnings*, 45).

Allow me to elaborate on this principle from more personal experiences. In another congregation there was a woman who caused much unrest among the members in our senior adults. Some of her ideas were good and worthy of consideration. She used the telephone to spread her thinking and, we discovered that she had the clout to tell some of our senior deacons how to vote on certain issues. Someone suggested that if she were invited to join the leadership committee she could share her ideas in the proper venue. I was appointed to ask her if she would be willing to serve in this capacity. The woman responded, "I don't want to be on the committee. I have more power being off it."

A fellow pastor found the power base to be in a small group of elders' wives. They discussed the church problems among themselves during coffee and instructed their husbands how to vote. To attempt to discover this power base, listen for the answers to these questions:

1. Identify a series of important decisions and examine whether individuals, groups, or both made them. How was power exerted in the decision-making process?

    a. Who really knows what happened?
    b. Who is the person others go to to get their information?

2. Who is the *inner circle* that makes the majority of the decisions?

    a. Is the *inner circle* made up through tradition, hierarchy, family, or other?

  b. Are there people on the outside desiring to get "in"?

  c. Is their inability to enter the circle real or perceived?

3. Is there an individual or group of people whose absence will cause the cancellation of a decision?

Questions about Beliefs

  There are three types of *belief systems* found in Christian organizations (Schaller, *Looking in the Mirror*, 59-60). Listen to hear the language that tells you how they want to be identified. First listen for the "language of law" – *legalism*. Is there a heavy emphasis on "rules, by-laws, policies, and strict standards?" This language will dominate the entire decision making process.

  A second category is "language of belief" – *ideology*. Listen to how members identify themselves; "We're a Bible-believing, Bible-teaching congregation." "We are a family church." "We believe in and support the family." "We favor. . ." It is important to understand that ideological congregations can be found in all the different theological realms. Just because a group speaks the *language of belief* does not mean they are *conservative*. The study of theology is a whole different field and hopefully you would not have accepted this position without that being well understood.

  The third category is the "language of relationships" – *behavioral*. These types of Christian organizations emphasize their relational closeness. They want to discuss how their leader is truly personable. They will tell about how he/she cares about people.

Questions about Finances

Regardless of what people say about organizational priorities, a study of its budget will reveal the truth. Here are some suggested facts which to observe.

1. What categories in the annual budget receive the largest percentage?

2. How much is budgeted *outward* – advertising, evangelism, etc.?

3. In a church, how much is budgeted for world mission? If any, what types of world missions are supported?

4. Are there any *special interest groups* written into the budget (e.g. Senior citizen programs, benevolence organizations)?

5. Is there any income from *unique* sources (e.g. estates, foundations, rental properties, mineral leases)? Does the presence of these funds affect current decisions?

Cultural Conclusions

Following the listening and observing sessions in homes and in meetings, take a couple of days to retreat, pray through and write out conclusions. However, resist the temptation to use judgmental terminology. The use of this kind of language will set itself in your mind and color any sharing of your findings.

1. For whom does this ministry exist?

2. If it were to face a major crisis tomorrow, how would it be handled?

3. Is the group locked into the past, plodding through the present, or anticipating the future?

4. On which age grouping do they seem to put the emphasis?

5. What person or group has the most power?

6. If you had a problem tomorrow, to whom would you go?

7. If you had a plan for tomorrow, to whom would you present it?

Mission Defined

Although a complete chapter will be presented on the subject of the mission statement, because it is a part of the cultural analysis, I would like to submit a definition at this point.

The purpose of an organization tells what it is to be: a church, a college, a crisis center, etc. In its objective, it joins many other organizations espousing the same purpose. Each organization, however, must put hands and feet on a *purpose statement* by defining how they desire to function to fulfill their purpose. In most cases this will separate them from other organizations with a similar purpose. The *mission statement*, therefore, is a unique proclamation of how the purpose will come to reality.

Values Defined

Our oldest son joined with an evangelism ministry to begin a new church. The leaders of that organization required that our son's team establish a list of core values upon which the ministry would be established. Since that time he has discovered that many people who have been drawn to the church have come in response to the core values posted on their website.

Much emphasis today is on an organization declaring up front their *core values*. This will become the bottom line of a culture study. All the goals, policies, strategies (or lack of them) are rooted in, and consistent with, these values. They are possibly the most powerful source of motivation built into an organization. They are the foundation on which its builds its image to the public as well as to its own people. *Core Values* provide direction for goals, set the limits on planning, form policy, and determine strategy. They are the moral boundaries to which the organization will hold or fold.

A famous study of organizations in the United States produced what is called *McKinsey 7-S Framework*. These are seven attributes used to examine organizational excellence. At the center of McKinsey's *7-S* diagram is an "S" for *shared values* which supports the other six: *structure, systems, style, staff, skills*, and *strategy* (Peters & Waterman,

46

In Search of Excellence, 7). Excellence in performance has to do with people being motivated by values.

Values make or break an organization. Not to choose any values is to have already chosen others. Values will surface in any organization and they will control its future. Thomas Watson, former CEO for IBM says:

> This then is my thesis: I firmly believe that any organization, in order to survive and achieve success, must have a sound set of beliefs on which it premises all its policies and actions. Next, I believe that the most important single factor in corporate success is faithful adherence to those beliefs... (Steiner, *Strategic Planning*, 151).

Integration of Cultural Components

This chapter has shown the development of culture from the innovative dream of the founder(s) through the determination of organizational values system. Over a period of time the dreams, purpose, mission, and values will rise to the top, either consciously or unconsciously, and they become the keys to the establishment and performance of an action plan or operational planning. The study of culture, coupled with a study of its assets, strengths, weaknesses, opportunities, and threats, will provide the foundation upon which the future will be built.

You are responsible to map out a plan for the future. The culture will determine that plan. If goals are not present, then the organization's cultural choice will be *maintenance* and this will kill the church, or cause it to lie dormant for years.

> If the organization is not suited to a strong culture, the culture may torpedo strategic thinking and action. On the one hand it could create a serious myopia among the [leaders] responsible for mapping out new directions, and, on the other hand, it could create a subtle but powerful resistance to change (Reimann & Wiener, "Corporate Culture," 48).

It is for these very reasons that you must begin by listening and appraising culture, mission, and values. When understood, you can build on them to create an action plan. This strategy would turn most ministries into growing bodies which represent God's culture, mission, and values to a lost world.

Chapter Three
Understanding Target Audience

Introduction

A famous cartoon shows a boy shoot an arrow at a blank wall. He then walks to the wall and draws a target around his arrow showing that he hit the center. As he walks away he tells his friends, "That is what I was shooting at all the time." Such is the way many organizations function.

God created the Church for people from all nations, tribes and tongues (Rev 5:9). To deny anyone would be a travesty of judgment. However, there is evidence that God's messengers brought an unchanging message in specific ways to specific people groups. The Apostle Paul claims that "To the weak I became weak, to win the weak. I have become all things to all men so that by all possible means I might save some (1 Co 9:22). Paul knew what he needed to do in order to target a particular audience. It would help you to do the same.

For this stage in leadership, there is an important equation to learn. It can guide in the understanding of the mission, and help you plan for its fulfillment. That formula is

Target Audience + Situational Analysis + Mission Statement = Strategic Plan (TA + SA + MS = SP)

Following this formula can help you demonstrate leadership and gain the confidence of those concerned about the future. The following is a step-by-step walk through this formula.

TA = Target Audience

Prior to my coming to the church in Glendale, AZ the congregation had fallen from an average attendance of 200 to thirty-five. The leaders and I began to chart on a map where members lived. We discovered that only four families lived within the Glendale city limits. We had a problem in that virtually no one from our immediate area was attending the church. This called for some hard decisions about who would be our *target audience*.

Understanding the Target Audience is a crucial step in setting a foundation for the vision and plan to fulfill it. Equally important to the understanding of a particular culture is to comprehend the makeup of the community it chooses to serve.

> Christians, more than any other group, should face the need to understand culture. This is an imperative. First, so that we might effectively penetrate our society with the gospel of Jesus Christ; and second, so that we may be truly Christian in the midst of a culture that is increasingly becoming antagonistic to our biblical presuppositions (Getz, *Sharpening the Focus of the Church*, 213).

There is no doubt that Jesus was a student of his culture. Jesus focused his ministry on the Jewish people rather than the Gentiles. We know, however, that the Gentiles were a part of His vision (Jn 10:16). Nevertheless, His immediate plan was to target the Jewish people who had long awaited His arrival.

The Apostle Paul also had a target audience. He stated that the Gospel was 'first for the Jews, then for the Gentile" (Ro 1:16). He knew his commission from the Lord was to target the Gentile part of God's vision (Gal 1:16). Paul was able to understand the concept of a target audience and adapt to it as the situation warranted. Once again, note his strategy:

> Though I am free and belong to no man, I make myself a slave to everyone, to win as many as possible. To the Jews I became like a Jew, to win the Jews. To those under the law I became like one under the law (though I myself am not under the law), so as to win those under the law. To those not having the law I became like one not having the law (though I am not free from God's law but am under Christ's law), so as to win those not having the law. To the weak I became weak, to win the weak. I have become all things to all men so that by all possible means I might save some. I do all this for the sake of the gospel, that I may share in its blessings.

> --1 Corinthians 9:19-23

This part of the strategic planning equation is to sharpen your sensitivity to your community culture and find the "Target Audience" at which your plans will be aimed. This is not to say that others will be left out. Even Peter, whose primary target was a Jewish audience, took the Gospel to Cornelius, a gentile (Ac 10:28). Philip left his preaching in Samaria to reach out to a man from Ethiopia (Ac 8:5, 26-34).

Most congregations do not understand their sur-rounding community.[3] One church where I served argued against the local demographics when they were presented. They still thought in terms of the neighborhood in which the building was built thirty years earlier. They said the statistic could not be true. Fortunately, the Chamber of Commerce (a highly respected non-government organization that monitors city growth and works to attract new businesses to that city) published its figures about a week later and the Chamber's figures confirmed what we presented. Often, the planning that does take place is aimed at the demographics of the people who attend its services every Sunday, people loyal to the church and willing to travel a distance to attend.

In many churches there seems to be little concern that the community might be changing. Churches refusing to accept the possibility of demographic shifts will face a difficult uphill task to keep its ministry alive. The same is true for a mission or parachurch organization. Learning *the marketplace* will help them remain relevant to the current society, and to fulfill the church's purpose. This requires getting to know people, understanding their languages (this goes beyond English, or whatever the tribal language might be, to the use of certain words and verbal concepts within the culture) and customs. Then, after taking this all in, design a way to relate with them.

There are people who will claim that demographic studies are a waste of time. These statistics are not easy to gather, and they are difficult to understand. Demographics are, however, a necessary tool for establishing relevancy in meeting the needs of a chosen community. To those who speak negatively concerning cultural studies, a famous church growth teacher says,

> To be sure, no one was ever saved by statistics; but then no one was ever cured by the thermometer to which the physician pays such close attention. X-ray pictures never knit a single broken bone, yet they are of considerable value to physicians in telling them how to put the two ends of a fractured bone together. Similarly, the facts of growth will not in themselves lead anyone to Christ. But they can be of marked value to any church which desires to know where, when, and how to carry on its work so that maximum increase of soundly Christian churches will result (McGavran, *Understanding Church Growth*, 84).

In the USA there are several sources from which information can be gathered to make an informed picture of any community. Similar resources are available in other countries. However, what follows are four common sources for demographic studies and suggestion on their use.

Denominational Headquarters

Many denominations retain people, or services, for the sole purpose of supplying this information to their constituency. If they do not, most are willing to assist a congregation in pulling together this helpful information. Some denominations are willing to pay for a professional demographics survey for any ministry committed to using the findings.

Secondary Sources

If the information is not available from denominational headquarters, then a leadership team can compile their own data. The first place to look for demographics is on the Internet. Larger cities have their own websites which provide a general picture of the city.

These statistics can be uncovered by obtaining reports from local agencies that use them in their business, in attracting new business, or applying for government grants. In the USA most cities have an organization called The Chamber of Commerce that works with local companies to attract people to come to their city to live and/or do business. If available, the local Chamber of Commerce, or any other Non-Government Organization (NGO) dealing with commerce and trade, is a wealth of information. Another source might be the principal of the local school. Most local libraries subscribe to the latest United States Bureau of Census reports. Someone in upper management for a retail establishment usually has access to very complete demographic studies done by their marketing department.

Through the use of this information, much more than the bare facts can be uncovered. Often they will help the researcher discover people's felt needs, reactions to political and social issues, changes in lifestyles, etc.

Companies Specializing in Demographics

A third source for obtaining demographic information is to contract with a company that specializes in demographic studies. These companies are in business to sell their studies of given areas of the country. You will generally contract for information concerning a specific neighborhood and be sent statistics, maps, charts, etc. If you can afford to subscribe to this service they will find it the fastest and most complete presentation of the facts available.

There are two drawbacks to subscribing to demographic information. First, it is costly. Even though they are extremely thorough, they tend to be more expensive than what the average religious organization will consider to be worth the cost. Secondly, there is no sense of value and ownership generated as when people work together to seek out the information about their own community and share their findings.

In the absence of all the above resources, you could do a *drive through* or *walk through* of your surroundings. With a list of characteristics you want to notice, travel through the area making observations.

Whatever source is used it is of vital necessity to know to whom the vision and plan will target. Before reaching out to your community you need to love that community, understand that community, and then ask yourself the hard question, "Am I able to reach this community?" or "What will have to change about me for that to happen?

Personal Community Surveys

Besides the necessity of compiling the demographics of the community, it is important to learn the heart of the people in the chosen Target Audience. Again, this is a place the average church in America is failing. Most have not stayed abreast of what is happening within their community. They are unaware of the thinking of the people and what is affecting their lives.

Localized feelings and how a church can best address them can be discovered by a well planned door-to-door survey. (Parachurch organizations can use a similar approach to their Target Audience.) Ask simple, non-threatening questions of those willing to respond. When Robert Schuller began the Garden Grove Community Church in California, he did so by sending workers throughout the community asking three questions: "Do you belong to a church?" "Are you active in your church?" And, "What do you believe a church should be doing to meet the community's needs?" From these responses, he built the great Crystal Cathedral (Schuller, Your Church Has Real Possibilities, 79-81).

During my seventeen years in Glendale, Arizona we did the demographic studies of the community three times to find what people were thinking. The first time we chose ten sections of thirty-five homes in different areas of the city. Workers went two-by-two to these homes and asked Schuller's questions. The response was overwhelmingly positive and the workers were ready to do it again. The top two responses of people's ideals for the church were: teach the Bible and have a strong youth program.

The second survey was done only in the neighborhood surrounding the church. Some seven hundred homes were contacted with the same questions. This time teaching the Bible was again the most frequent response; however, helping families was second.

The third survey was done by ten people within the congregation who went to the people in their neighborhood. This produced nearly one hundred responses from a cross-section of the community. This time we asked specific questions about our church: "Do you know where it is located?" "Do you know what it stands for?" "Have you ever attended a service or activity there?" "What do you think the church should be doing?" We were pleasantly surprised to discover how well we were known throughout the community.

Setting Your Sights

Once information has been gathered, it can be assimilated into a picture of the target. Saddleback Community Church in Irvine, California, has put a name to its target. "Saddleback Sam" is a person with whom the Saddleback leadership is well acquainted. He is a compilation of all that the church must focus as their target (Warren, *Purpose-Driven Church*, 169). In the Glendale, AZ church the leadership developed "Glendale Gus." This mythical person was twenty-eight years of age, married with two children ages five and three. Both he and his wife had some college training; however, they had not graduated. They worked in Phoenix, but lived in Glendale because of lower housing costs; and most were buying their first house. They were very interested in family activities, with a particular penchant for team sports and camping.

Later, when the demographics were updated, our leadership team renamed our target "Glendale Gunther and Gloria" ("Gus" was changed to "Gunther" because of a strong Russian/German heritage in the early history of the city). Their designation of a couple was a result of our need to

57

realize two facts: there were women in our target audience and the majority of people in our target area were married.

Once all the community facts have been gathered and the audience has been defined, the ministry must refer to them as they focus their planning so that decisions are made in context. New programs will be added as a result of this community diagnosis. Therefore, it is important to obtain a realistic view of the context within which the church is centered.

This information, however, is not an end in itself: it is a means to an end. Existing activities and goals should be evaluated on the basis of this target audience. On the basis of "Glendale Gunther and Gloria," the congregation began a very effective pre-school (the target was those who were family-oriented and had a child three years old). Because of *Gunther and Gloria's* love for team sports, the church put re-newed efforts into a sports outreach.

Morning worship services were re-evaluated through the eyes of the Target Audience and some major changes had to be made. The leadership took a new look at how the educational ministry was structured and the condition of the rooms. The nursery was painted bright colors and the pic-tures on the wall were lowered to a child's eye level. Most churches would be amazed at what could be done when they begin to look through the eyes of their target audience. As a result, the Glendale church saw many families introduced to Christ and make life-changing decisions.

Therefore, whenever a new direction or program is planned, first seek to understand the Target Audience and how they will respond. Ministries grow the fastest among homogeneous groups – groups that share culture, class, age, or ethnicity. If leadership is not aware of the cultural make-up of each group, they will never be able to grow in the pattern of the New Testament church. Parachurch organizations must understand the people they desire to reach. Therefore, a ministry that does not analyze its Target Audience cannot truly know whether or not it is meeting people's needs with the gospel. A so-called *Christian organization* that does not bring the gospel to meet need is not in the business of ministry, and their mission will never be clearly defined.

Chapter Four
Understanding Mission

Mission Defined

Abraham Lincoln is quoted as saying, "If we could first know where we are, and whither we are tending, we could then better judge what to do and how to do it" (Steiner, *Strategic Planning*, 124-125). The third initials of the strategic planning equation (MS) stands for *Mission Statement*. The second initials SA will be discussed later in this chapter; however, it is necessary to gain a sense of direction before performing a Situational Analysis (SA).

It is imperative for a Christian organization to decide whom they hope to reach and how they desire to accomplish that ministry. This is where purpose meets demographics and culture to determine *mission*. A written statement of the proposed mission sets the direction and provides the rallying point for action. Jesus Christ is the Chief Cornerstone (Eph 2:19-22) and every aspect of our operation must be measured against His life and instructions.

A well-written mission statement answers the question of why this ministry exists. It is the same for a pastor, missionary, parachurch CEO or cell group leader. A well-written mission statement calls people to goal-centered action. In every person there is a desire to make a difference; this statement becomes an invitation to fulfill that need to contribute. Without a well thought out sense of mission it is very possible that you will begin to lose key people who desire action that is aimed at a purpose.

Purpose and Mission

When I came to be the new pastor in Glendale, AZ, I discovered that the leadership had no idea that their thinking had to go beyond purpose. They knew they were planted to be a conservative evangelical church in the growing suburb. However, other than weekly services, they had no thought about how that was put into action. *Purpose* is a simple statement of why an organization believes it exists – to be a church, a youth camp, a missionary organization, or other. *Mission*, however, puts feet and hands to the *purpose*. *Vision* sees what those feet and hands can/needs do.

The Glendale Church was created for the purpose of being a part of the greater Body of Christ, yet representing a particular theological position in its community. The leaders knew the church was supposed to grow. They had a dream with no definition or plan. Had they been asked, any of the leaders would have told you, "Our mission is to reach people for Christ." However, how that was to happen and what to do when it did happen was outside their thinking.

We planned a twenty-four hour leadership retreat for the purpose of writing a mission statement. I have never experienced a retreat so quickly develop into open warfare as the men refused to accept the fact that we were operating without a mission. They took the suggestion as an attack on their leadership. When we finally got them calmed down and defined what we were talking about, we then endured a time of finger-pointing seeking to blame those responsible. It was a difficult weekend; however, we did finally emerge with a shared statement of the church's mission that guided the church's planning for years to come.

Our next step following the mission retreat gave birth to *Glendale Gunther and Gloria* (our Target Audience). Once we understood this young family that made up most of our community we were able to begin to create a vision of ways to reach them. That vision brought birth to a preschool and sports program designed to help us fulfill our mission and purpose. These targeted ministries resulted in many young couples coming to Christ and becoming a part of the church.

Many Christian organizations wander without direction. For instance, many churches understand their *purpose* to be a church of some denominational or non-denominational brand. Their *mission*, however, is simply to be open next Sunday. For many church attendees this is not a problem because as long as the doors are open, the environment is comfortable and the preacher delivers a decent sermon, they are happy.

A friend of mine was asked to consult with a stagnated church. He met with the leadership and asked them to submit in writing what they believed to be the church's mission. From the ten people in attendance, the consultant received back eight totally different ideas of the church's mission. And, most of those were more statements of *purpose* rather than *mission*.

All strategic planning is based upon the mission statement. There can be no vision or master plan for growth and/or change until the organization is able to assess core beliefs about accomplishing its purpose for existence. Without such an assessment, they remain in a maintenance mentality, at best. Enthusiasm and attendance decline for lack of planning or goals.

The mission statement, therefore, is a very formative and foundational document. Its purpose is to function as a plumb line which all future planning is measured against; making sure all is in line with its purpose.

Jesus' Mission

Our Lord, Jesus Christ, established a mission statement for His ministry. Based on His purpose to "seek and save the lost," Jesus, as He spoke to the synagogue leaders in Nazareth (Lk 4:18-19), quoted Isaiah's prophecy concerning the mission of the Messiah.

> The Spirit of the Sovereign LORD is on me,
> because the LORD has anointed me
> to preach good news to the poor.
> He has sent me to bind up the brokenhearted,
> to proclaim freedom for the captives
> and release from darkness for the prisoners,
> to proclaim the year of the LORD's favor . . .

-- Isaiah 61:1-2

Recognizing that Jesus functioned with a mission statement that He readily expressed, gives us all the more reason why we should be eager to establish a statement for our own direction, making sure that it is in line with His.

In essence the mission statement is saying, "This is why we believe God has put us here, this is the task He has given us and we will cease to exist rather than give up our mission." Before this can be completed, however, it is important for you and your people to have a thorough understanding of the present situation. This brings us to the second set of initials in our equation for grasping a vision and doing strategic planning.

The Situational Analysis

Describing Situational Analysis

Situational Analysis (SA) is a tool to create an understanding of all the forces currently effecting an organization. I have used this tool for churches, camps, mission teams and parachurch organizations. This audit of present conditions is referred to as a "SWOT Analysis" – an acronym for the Strengths, Weaknesses, Opportunities, and Threats that affect planning. An important goal of strategic planning is to discover future opportunities and threats so as to make plans to exploit or avoid them. Earlier I quoted leadership author Max DePree who believes "the first responsibility of a leader is to define reality" (DePree, *Leadership Is an Art*, 9). This is the exact purpose of the SWOT Analysis. Therefore, it is a critical step to the process of implementing a vision to fulfill mission and purpose.

In an existing organization that has no mission statement, the Situational Analysis draws a picture of how the people see themselves and where they need to be headed. The study helps to surface the threats to existence and generates an understanding of the needs of the Target Audience.

A new leader does not begin with a complete long-range program ready to be kicked-off the first day on the job. You, as a new head, cannot arrive with a pre-planned agenda. Instead, you must begin by finding ways to awaken the people to their mission and long range plan. To attempt to establish a plan before the weaknesses, opportunities, threats, and strengths are recognized is unsound leadership.

How Situational Analysis Is Conducted

The situational analysis is best conducted in a series of meetings planned specifically for this study. I have conducted analyses both in a retreat setting and in consecutive nightly or weekly meetings. Careful preplanning and follow through maximizes the effectiveness these gatherings. The following is a guideline for individual sessions.

Each session should be led with a *light* atmosphere where the attendees fell comfortable and free to share. Welcome each individual with excitement and thanks for their attendance.

Session 1

A good cross-section of leadership within the organization should be invited – women, youth, music, home fellowships, etc. A questionnaire for studying the situational analysis should be given to each participant prior to this original meeting. It should be a piece of paper divided into four sections. Each section should be headlined with one of the SWOT areas. Strengths and Weaknesses are *internal* realities within the leadership team, facilities and/or programs. Opportunities and Threats are *external* realities that can assist or challenge organizational mission – changing demographics, traffic changes, etc. The participants need to have a clear understanding of the difference between *internal* and *external* realities.

Before their arrival the participants should list their thoughts under each section and bring it to the meeting. It is best to seat the attendees into groups of four or five with each table including a leader who has been briefed prior to the session. Beginning with *Strengths*, each table will compile a single list of their evaluations. As members share around their table, encourage the leader to ask, "Do you have anything to add to our list that is not already on it?" This is a time for *listing*; *do not allow any discussion* concerning someone's suggested item. This saves much time as it weeds out duplicate items. It is important that every person sees their thoughts written on the paper.

After a set amount of time, allow the groups to share their findings with the other tables. Similar to what happened on a small scale, as each thought is shared it is written so everyone can see. Ask each group to only share items that have not yet been listed

.

After you have your compiled list from each table, repeat the process for each area of the SWOT Analysis. The purpose is to bring to the surface critical issues that presently reside within the minds of your people, to identify the key trends, forces, and problems that have a potential impact on the formulation and implementation of your vision. When everyone has shared, thank them and assure them that each item listed will be reviewed and presented at the next meeting.

Session 2

Before this session, have the four lists printed for each participant to have in hand. Some people might want to add to them; however, be careful that this does not become a long process. Have the team vote to prioritize each list, beginning with Strengths. If this initial list is long, it may need to be narrowed down by a series of votes. During the first round tell the people that they can vote on the ten items they believe to be the greatest strengths of the ministry (if the list is short, reduce it to five). Erase those that received few or no votes and vote again, instructing the participants to vote on five (or three). I have had situations where a list contained eighty items and required a third or fourth vote to get the list to the *top ten*. Depending on the number of strengths presented on the original list, narrow it to the top five to ten and present them as "The Greatest Strengths of Our Ministry." Celebrate these.

Once the list of Strengths has been compiled, continue to the next column. However, be prepared for what will happen when the list of Weaknesses is presented. The human mind concentrates more on weaknesses than on strengths. Therefore, it is not uncommon to have a list of Weaknesses that exceeds Strengths by two or three times. Do not let this throw your people. Be ready to explain that this is normal. Proceed to vote as you did on strengths to bring the list to the top five or ten. Then do the same for Opportunities and Threats.

When the SWOT Analysis is complete it gives a very clear picture of the heart and mind of the people. Take care to save these lists for future reference when doing strategic planning.

Asset Mapping

A second process that would allow you to *define reality* is known as *asset mapping*. In the last section we noted that in the midst of doing a SWOT Analysis leaders have to prepare themselves for the fact that the list of *weaknesses* can be three to four times longer than *strengths*. Asset mapping is a way of studying conditions that attempts to put the emphasis on what God has been and is doing within the community, rather than focusing on *weaknesses* or *deficiencies*. "This deficiency focus is usually described as a concern about the needs of local members. And these needs are understood to be the problems, shortcomings, maladies and dilemmas of people" (Russell, *Intro to Asset Mapping*, p. 1). Focusing on deficiencies will prevent growth as "People are seen as lacking instead of having something to offer. What we fail to realize is that in our communities it's the capabilities of the individuals that build the community and not the deficiencies" (Russell, p. 1).

Asset mapping is an intentional look at the people, facilities and ministries in a way that asks the questions, "What is good?" "What do we have on which we can build?" To lead your leadership in this evaluation you will need to create a list of areas within the organization that you want to explore – leadership, children's ministries, youth ministries, worship, orphan care, medical clinic etc. Your list will depend on the community in which you are located.

I often lead exercises in team building in which the teams have to make a listing of their resources to solve a particular problem. It is amazing to me that few teams ever ask the question, "Does anyone have any training or experience with this problem?" One of the most overlooked resources in an evaluation process is people. We look at our finances and facilities, but not our people. Begin by asking the question, "Who has God brought together for this time?" If we believe there are no coincidences with God, then we have to believe that God has gathered the people needed to face the current situation and upon whom you can plan the future.

Make your findings a part of the notebook suggested in chapter eleven of this book. However, this is not just information for records. If this study gets hidden in a book, you will lose integrity as a leader. This is meant to be a listing of assets that God has already provided upon which you can lead your people into the future. The resources of people coupled with what God has provided in facilities as well as those found in the community, are valuable assets that you already have in hand.

Guidelines for Writing a Mission Statement

Make It Simple

I was asked to consult with a mid-sized American church. As I talked to the leadership, I asked them if they had a mission statement. They proudly announced that they had one and handed me a three-ringed binder with over thirty pages of *mission statement*. After a short conversation the pastor told me that they had a difficult time getting people to read it.

If a mission statement contains too much detail, it becomes counterproductive. It stifles creativity and can create division by people who delight in legalities. If it is too wordy, it will not give a clear call for people to follow. Most authors believe that a mission statement should never be longer than a paragraph. Others would allow one page. None would allow the statement to continue beyond this length.

Try to avoid the common mistake of making your mission statement a collection of good intentions. Simply and clearly state the direction in which you desire the people go. Remember the words of the Apostle Paul, "If the trumpet does not sound a clear call, who will get ready for battle?" (1 Co 14:8). He asked the Colossians to pray that he might clearly present his message (Col 4:4); this should also be our prayer in both preaching and leading.

Make It Flexible

The purpose of *making it simple* is to insure that it is not so precise that it suppresses creativity. A balanced mission statement will be flexible enough to encourage free thinking, but specific enough to keep the mission on track. The paradox of the mission statement is that it is straight, yet it will bend to include new ministries and programs.

Jesus' mission statement, for instance, carried His mandate for ministry, "The Spirit of the Lord is on me to preach...to proclaim...to release" (Lk 4:18-19). It does not use any exclusive language to tell Jesus what He cannot do, or how and where He is to accomplish His mission. Yet, the statement is specific enough to become a plumb line to His ministry to keep Him on track – good news, freedom, recovery, release and to proclaim the year of God's favor.

A mission statement that announces "We intend to evangelize our community with door-to-door calling every Tuesday evening" will find itself stifled if Tuesday becomes a problem. It could also be a dilemma if people refuse to participate in "door-to-door calling." A church that expresses its intentions to "to promote an atmosphere of evangelism through a variety of outreach opportunities," will not be stifled. Yet, they will know that evangelism is to be their mission. Because it must be balanced, creating a church's mission statement will take time and patience.

Create Ownership among Leaders

While I was leading a workshop on "Writing A Mission Statement for Your Church," a man proclaimed, "This is a waste of time. I have written five mission statements for my congregation and they have not accepted any of them." I asked him, "Did you ever consider *leading them* to write a mission statement?" He returned a blank stare and answered, "No."

When talking to the person in charge of the convocation program at a Christian college, he shared how the students would not participate. I asked if a mission statement for the services had been written. He replied, "Every faculty person for the past five years who has been assigned to plan the convocations has begun with a mission statement." I asked, "Have the students, for whom it is required, ever been involved in the writing of the statement?" You have already guessed the answer.

As I shared earlier about the twenty-four hour retreat for our church, as difficult as it was, when we were done, "the leaders owned it." They left that weekend claiming, "This is

<u>our</u> mission statement." In the years to follow, *they* would bring it up as a point of reference to ideas. A mission statement that has no ownership is good only for wasting time, paper, and ink.

There is a frequent mistake made by people who want to be leaders. They agonize over several different mission statements, only for the people to think, "That is not our mission. You go ahead if you want to, but don't expect our support." Leaders who fail to involve their people in the writing of the mission statement will find themselves very much alone in its fulfillment. The "performance of the group is the only real proof of leadership" (DePree, *Leadership Jazz*, 206). In two different books by the same author we find these confirmations of the need of *ownership*:

> Many organizations have a mission statement, but typically people aren't committed to it because they aren't involved in developing it; consequently it's not part of the culture (Covey, *Principle-Centered Leadership*, 165).

> Without involvement, there is no commitment. Mark it down, asterisk it, circle it, and under-line it. *No involvement, no commitment* (Covey, *The Seven Habits*, 143).

Components of an Effective Mission Statement

Finalizing a mission statement is your responsibility. You are listening to the people to find that common thread that weaves through the Situational Analysis and the study of the Target Audience. You are hearing what people are saying about meaning. You are attempting to understand what they hope to accomplish. You are listening so that you can lead them in a common direction. You are helping them put their ideas into writing.

Who Are We?

The first component of the mission statement is a statement of who we are, where we are, and our dream to bring meaning in this need. There is more than one church in most villages and cities; there are many parachurch organizations with similar purposes. Therefore, a mission statement should set one apart from the others. Be careful not begin with, "We are a church that wants..." Begin by proudly speaking the ministry's name and location, "First Church of Your Town, Kansas exists to..." "Good News Missions in Harare, Zimbabwe exists to . . ."

What We Are About

I had the privilege to work with the board of a mission that had a unique calling. The missionary/founder had a firm idea of what the mission was to be. He could not, however, explain it to others. His board served because they loved him and his wife and were committed to them. No one, however, could explain exactly what the mission did. During two very long sessions, we wrestled the dream out of the founder's thinking, mixed it with some insights from the board members and put it on a chalkboard. Everyone unanimously agreed to the statement, including the founder. When the people finally saw it, there was a big sigh of relief. "Now," stated a long-time board member, "I can finally explain to my church what this mission is all about." They now could go tell others what they were all about. During the next year they were able to become not only supporters, but active advocates of the mission's mission.

"Vision and mission must always be consistent and complementary. A vision inspires the mission and the mission implements the vision" (McKenna, *Power to Follow*, 93). In writing a mission statement, lead the people to visualize what they want to be, and put their dreams into words. This is done because they will use this statement to explain who they are to themselves and outsiders.

How We Are Going To Do It

The body of the mission statement is by far the most important part. It is a simple flexible statement that explains what a ministry desires to be. There is a need, however, for some statements about how they are going to attempt to fulfill the mission. Following the body of your mission statement there can be a listing of *bullets* that begin, "With God's help, we hope to accomplish our mission through..." These bullets are very specific and very short statements of belief. For example, "We hope to accomplish this through: Preaching the Bible as God's answer to today's needs; and promoting and encouraging evangelism as every member's responsibility." Again, brevity is the key. These bullets should be no more than one sentence in length and there should be no more than seven to a mission statement.

The Final Draft

Based on the above understanding of a mission statement, the final draft will have these components:

Who we are (our purpose for being – a church, a camp, a mission, etc)

Where we are (our location – our town, state or country)

What is our goal for this mission (what sets us apart from other similar organizations)

How we hope to accomplish this mission (a listing of ways to fulfill the mission – remember, simple and flexible.

How we will know that we are accomplishing our mission (be careful not to restrict yourself by using numbers, or other measuring devices)

Never include anything in a statement of mission that the people are not willing to back up with action.

As the strategic questions listed above (who, where, what, how, etc.) are considered, take time to discuss each question thoroughly. Write and rewrite the statement. Let the group suggest words and phrase alternatives. This will become a semantic wrestling match. This is okay as it is a part of the process that creates ownership. The process is as important as the final product. The exciting result in this process is that the team creates its own strategic analysis. They experience firsthand what it takes to gather data, structure it, present it in a formal setting, answer questions about it, revise it, and draw conclusions. The analysis has tremendous credibility because it was developed by the people themselves (McKenna, *Power to Follow*, 54).

Once the rough draft is completed, the people should be dismissed until the next day. They will be mentally exhausted by this time. In the meantime, the rough draft can be cleaned up and copies made for the next session. Some of the sentence structure and language flow may need to be corrected. You may even want to bring back your sugges-tions for the next meeting. Remember, however, this is to be *their* mission statement, not yours.

At the next meeting, after everyone has had time to renew their thinking processes, present them with the clean copies. During the break, many of them will have thought through some of the items. Their suggestions will be impor-tant.

> "Repeated revision will streamline both wording and content. The final draft may be similar or even the same as the existing purpose statement, but going through the process is an essential part of any major change" (Anderson, *Dying For Change*, 162-163).

By the time this session is completed, the group should have a mission statement and the excitement to begin planning to fulfill it.

Share Your Results
The next step is to plan with the statement creators a strategy for sharing it with the people. Publish it, teach it,

share it in meetings, and help leadership put it into a short speech to share at a moment's notice. If you are a pastor, refer to it often in sermons and newsletter articles; give it a priority location on the church's website. Hang it on a banner where all can see. Share it often until it begins to infiltrate people's thinking and begins to be a part of the new culture.

Conclusion

The writing of a mission statement and the creation of ownership will be one of the most important foundational accomplishments of your first year. It must not be rushed. Build it out of the cultural studies and teamwork. Involve as many people as possible. When this task is completed – celebrate. Your leadership, however, is just beginning!

Chapter Five
Picturing the Future

Introduction

Before David faced Goliath, David had a picture in mind of just what was going to happen on the battlefield. As he approached the giant, David told Goliath in detail what the results of the day would be (1 Sa 17:45 - 47). David had surveyed the situation, visualized the end results, planned accordingly and now moved into action. What David had in mind is what is referred to as a *scenario* – a clear picture of the end results. That is your next step in the strategic planning process.

Vision and *mission* come together in this written description of what you expect to happen over a given period of time. It is a completed plan of long-term objectives which represent what the church wants to become at that future point. We have mentioned Jesus' vision of seeing the gospel being spread throughout the entire world (Mt 28:19). If Jesus had written a scenario, it would have read something like this: "I envision the gospel having spread to Ethiopia, Ephesus, throughout the Galatian peninsula, and missionaries working in Rome." A *scenario* is similar to goals, only without the specific numbers, dates, and assignment of responsibility.

If you are following the guidelines of this strategy you are working hard to define reality – to obtain a correct picture of the present situation. You are continuing to listen and observe to discover the culture of the church. Demographic studies have been compiled to give an awareness of the Target Audience and the leadership team has a well-written shared mission statement. Now it is time to dream about what it will look like with all these components working together.

What needs to be done at this point of the leadership strategy, before the specifics of a long-range plan, is what Steven Covey calls, to "begin with the end in mind."

> To begin with the end in mind means to start with a clear understanding of your destination. It means to know where you're going so that you better understand where you are now and so that the steps you take are always in the right direction (Covey, Seven Habits, 98).

There are many excuses for why an organization is not reaching its potential. Some even blame it on unspiritual leaders; others say, "The devil is holding us back." However, the devil does not need to work hard if the people are set in maintenance thinking. Most churches are the same today as they were twenty years ago because no one has ever been able to convince members that they have a bright future. No one has ever helped them paint a picture of what they could become. No one has helped them plan a systematic course of achieving the dream. In such cases, the forces that would nullify the church's impact upon its community do not have to work hard at all. One author observes,

> It is easily observed that most churches do not engage in such systematic long-range planning. Perhaps this is one reason why the

church has not been able to reach and change society more effectively. Many local churches operate on hand-to-mouth planning. They consider the pressing problems of the moment at each board meeting without placing them in proper perspective in relation-ship to either past or future. The result is that expediency of the shallowest kind determines most decisions (Lindgren, *Purposeful Administration,* 226).

In contrast, "a well-defined, broadly-owned, and sharply-focused dream of ministry provides organizational power" (Dale, *Pastoral Leadership* , p. 65). It will attract people, keep people centered on the target, and provide the sense of meaning for which many people are looking.

You and your leadership team must decide if you are going to be *thermostats* or *thermometers.* A *thermometer* simply allows you to know the current temperature. A *thermostat* sets and controls the temperature in an oven or building. Simply to react to current stimuli (thermometer) is to plan for status quo where most leadership topics revolve around "fire fighting" – reacting to current problems. The creation of the *scenario* explained in this chapter is like building a thermostat into your leadership meetings that will impact the present and future conditions. The goal is to become proactive, rather than reactive, to help leaders pursue goals, rather than always responding to daily pressures. Leaders need to be intentional, rather than habitual, function by design, rather than by whim.

Steps to Writing a Scenario

Review of Situational Analysis

One of the most enjoyable meetings I ever led was when we gathered leaders together for this activity. What began as an evening of fun and laughter ended with huge dreams of possibilities, most of which were eventually realized.

Never in any part of the planning allow the work that went into the Situational Analysis get away from you. People thought long and hard to come up with these lists; do not just file them away. Some people put their hopes and reputations on the line to mention and vote for some of the items, believing you will do something with them. To leave the work and information behind would be a major setback to your leadership integrity.

Brainstorming

"Dreams are the roots for plans. Plans are the fruit of dreams" (Dale, *To Dream Again*, 147). Therefore, the next step is to get groups together and allow for dreaming – better known as *brainstorming*. Remind the participants that there are two rules in brainstorming: no idea is wrong and no idea is to be discussed at this time. I find it helpful to give each group a blank piece of paper with this paragraph at the top:

> Five years have passed and everything in . . .
> (insert your ministry name) has been
> happening without any major problems.
> Imagine you are a magazine reporter whose

editor has heard about the exciting events in your organization and has sent you to write a report. What will your report say? (Write as if you were reporting five years from now.)

It is my experience that people left to dream in such a way gain new enthusiasm for what can happen. Martin Luther King Jr. caught the attention of an entire nation by shouting, "I have a dream!" Properly used, the scenario can do the same for any organization. A vision of *what can be* creates a spark of energy for you and those who follow you. This makes this scenario important enough to spend the time. That is why an effort is made to get everyone involved in picturing the future. Yes, you could do this so much easier by yourself, but it will be so extremely difficult to create ownership of the resulting vision. Without a shared vision, people just work day-to-day and expect **you** to be working on **your** vision.

What to Avoid

In India I teach a seminary class called, "The Effective Church." The syllabus is based on Rick Warren's excellent book, *The Purpose-Driven Church*. The final examination for that class always has the question, "Explain the Page 68 Principle." On page sixty-eight Warren writes, "While you cannot grow a church trying to be someone else, you *can* grow a church by using principles someone else discovered and then filtering them through your personality and context . . . God has a custom ministry for every church" (Warren, *Purpose-Driven Church*, p. 68). The key phrase in this quote is "filtering them" – making them fit your situation.

This is becoming a recurrent theme. There is a great temptation facing Christian leaders to study the great leadership successes and try re-creating their programs. It is important that each organization finds a niche that fits within its culture. That is the purpose of this strategy – to find and fulfill the ministry God has given the local community. A successful Christian leader warns that "clones almost never work. More likely what worked once will probably have to be reworked; it's in a different place at a different time" (Johnson, *Leadership Magazine*, p.68).

There is, however, a wealth of information to be gained from your study of *success stories* and their leaders. It is good for you to study these and bring home ideas for planning. But to implant them is harmful. "Most effective strategies are 'homemade,' laboriously and prayerfully hammered out for a given time and place" (Ellis, *Church On Purpose*, 162).

A second stumbling block to avoid in writing a scenario is "unmeasurable objectives." Encourage your people to dream in numbers. Instead of saying, "We will have increased our missions budget," write, "We are excited because our missions budget is twenty per cent above where it was five years ago." Instead of saying, "We have grown significantly," write "We have grown by 100 new converts a year for the past five years."

Review

Once the scenario has been written, it is important that it be reviewed to make sure it is workable. The first point of review is to go back to the equation for a vision. Does it match the Mission Statement written by the people? Is everything in line with what they said they wanted to be? Secondly, does it answer the needs raised in the Situational Analysis? Are opportunities being met and threats being addressed? Are strengths being utilized to compensate for weaknesses? Thirdly, does it show impact on the Target Audience? Will this dream excite the people it is designed to reach? Does it give a clear sense of purpose that captivates and rallies the people? Will it weld them together, move them harmoniously in the same direction, and guide their actions? If it does, then a good scenario has been created on which to begin strategic planning for the future.

The following is an example of how a *scenario* might read as each paragraph shares what will be happening five years from now if every aspect of the vision is fulfilled:

> First Church of Your Town, Kansas has been a part of our community since 1948; however, according to Lead Pastor John Smith, the last five years have been some of the best. When Pastor Smith came to Your Town six years ago, he began a study of the community and led the congregation to see a vision of what could be done to help the people here in Your Town and around the world.

> First Church has added two new pastors to the staff. Three years ago a Youth Pastor was called to build a program designed specifically for teen-aged youth. Under his leadership the group of thirty middle and high school students has participated in cleanup projects

throughout the city; they maintain a garden at the Your Town Elementary School from which they share their harvest with families in need. For the past three years the youth have traveled to Mexico to build homes for people living in the slums.

Last year First Church hired its first Worship Pastor. Calling on a background in music, sound and video production, he is leading the church's vision to become cutting-edge in all these departments. In the next year there will be some major remodeling in the church's auditorium and new equipment will be installed.

I also found that brightly painted rooms greet the children who attend First Church. Ann Hampton, a long-time member of the congregation, has added beautiful murals in some of the younger meeting areas.

Pastor Smith reports that seventy-five new people have begun attending First Church in the past five years. New church attendees have the opportunity to take classes in the Bible, personal growth and leadership.

SECTION 2

SECOND LEADERSHIP RESPONSIBILITY

INFLUENCING OWNERSHIP

Chapter Six
Leadership Is Influence

Introduction

A vision of possibilities was only the beginning of what Jesus had to share with His disciples as He prepared to make His final ascension into heaven. In His closing statement to The Twelve, He directed them to "make disciples" as they went into every nation (Mt 28:19). In order to fulfill His vision, they would have to encounter people's culture, religious thinking, and lifestyle. They were to challenge listeners with the message and mission of the Christ. The goal was to bring people everywhere into the ranks of *believers*. They were to become learners of a new way of thinking and a new lifestyle.

The act of "making disciples" is an act of *influence*. The result of this act is *ownership*. Jesus wants people to take hold of the Kingdom in such a way that it impacts their life. He desires us to feel a responsibility for its continuation. His plan depends on you and me influencing people to become disciples.

Once again, Jesus is not merely giving us His final earthly command. He is demonstrating the second leadership responsibility that cannot be delegated. It is not enough to grasp a vision of possibilities. Mission Statements and scenarios are only the beginning. It is not enough to hold in your hand a file folder containing all the information gathered from studies of demographics, cultures and Situational Analyses. You, as the leader, have the responsibility to influence others to act upon what they now know.

Influence Ownership of the Vision

In his letter to the young evangelist, Paul told Timothy, "Here is a trustworthy saying: If any one sets his heart on being an overseer, he desires a noble task" (1 Tm 3:1). It is generally understood that an *overseer* is a leader in the local church. Therefore, Paul is saying that it is not bad; in fact, it is *noble* to desire to be a leader. But, what does that mean? Is leadership a position of importance where a person is either a decision maker or consultant; or is it when an individual steps to the front of the group and says, "Let's go this way!"?

As we come to the second *leadership responsibility*, we will look at why it is biblically honorable to influence people, and then examine some suggestions as to how to make a lasting impact that perpetuates ownership of the vision.

During my undergraduate training in Christian Ministries I took a class entitled, "Church Administration." In eight years of college and seminary this one class was the only one offered that had any semblance of leadership training. The professor instructed us in how to plan weddings, funerals, stewardship programs, how to edit a newsletter and how to be ready to handle the directives of the board. Because this class was not indigenous to one college, I find that many Christian organizations are hampered by leaders and board members who were never trained "to lead." They have had a few lessons on qualifications and how to be a spiritual helper, but not in how to *lead* people.

Leadership is the glue that holds any organization together. If it is not present or is inactive then the body begins to drift apart.

> Leadership is not optional; it is essential. Essential for motivation and direction. Essential for evaluation and accomplishment. It is the one ingredient essential for the success of any organization. Take away leadership and it isn't long before confusion replaces vision (Swindoll, *Leadership*, 7).

Your leadership, therefore, becomes key to the success of the ministry you have chosen to head. You cannot stand quietly in the background. However, you cannot force yourself to the front. The right to influence people to follow must be earned.

Careful scrutiny of biblical leadership and modern leadership literature makes a very clear point: As the leader, it is your responsibility to *influence* people in such a way that they become stronger, wiser and more capable to someday be leaders. Allow me to enforce my point:

> At the risk of oversimplifying, I'm going to resist a long, drawn-out definition and settle on one word. It's the word *influence*. If you will allow me two words - *inspiring influence* (Swindoll, *Leadership*, 19).

Leadership is an action-oriented, interpersonal influencing process (Dale, *Pastoral Leadership*, 14).

Leadership is a relationship between a person exerting influence and those who are influenced (E. P. Hollander, quoted by Butt, *Velvet-Covered Brick*, 58).

Leadership is any influence any person has on an individual or group to meet its needs or goals for the glory of God (LePeau, *Paths of Leadership*, 10).

"Influence" is defined as, "The act or the power of producing an effect without apparent force or direct authority, hence, power arising from situation, character, wealth, etc." (*Webster's New Collegiate Dictionary*, rev. ed., 1960). This definition is packed with meaning and is the message I desire to share in this chapter. We will spend more time on the components of this definition as you work through this chapter.

Biblical Examples of Leadership by Influence

While I was a student in seminary a guest lecturer made the comment that for us, as preachers, to try to get the congregation to follow our vision was an act of pride; and, pride is a sin. Our responsibility is to tend the sheep, and nothing else. I wrestled with that statement for some time; and then concluded that it did not match what I was reading in Scripture. Even the shepherd makes decisions and *influences* his sheep to follow him to green pastures and quiet waters (Ps 23:2).

In every leadership narrative in Scripture we find an individual who is attempting to influence the thinking of others. God commissioned leaders to go forth and change the way people thought about their present situation and/or their relationship to Him. Biblical leaders were mind changers, trend setters, revival starters, and deliverers – all of which demand *influencing* people to a new way of thinking.

When God sent Moses to Egypt it was to influence the thinking of Pharaoh to let the Israelites leave the country (Ex 6:11). Moses had to influence the Jews to follow him out of Egypt. Moses gave God's direction to Eleazar, the priest; to Joshua, and to all family heads of the Israelite tribes (Nu 32:28). Joshua, Moses' protégé, followed in his footsteps as a leader, giving directions, sharing vision, and setting policy. Joshua demanded a choice from the people, "Then choose for yourselves this day whom you will serve. . . . But as for me and my household, we will serve the LORD" (Jos 24:15).

Nehemiah entered the broken city of Jerusalem and after examining the ruins helped the people believe they could rebuild. As a result, the people were influenced to do the necessary work (Ne 2:18). As problems arose, he ministered to his people and continually encouraged them to work, "Don't be afraid of them. Remember the Lord, who is great and awesome, and fight for your brothers, your sons and your daughters, your wives and your homes" (Ne 4:14). Nehemiah faced down the leaders who were using their position to usurp the final bit of money from the people. He caused the unscrupulous leaders to change their minds and respond to the needs of the individual (Ne 5:10-11). On every page of the record of Nehemiah's leadership, we see him influencing people.

As we turn to the New Testament, the practice of leadership by influence does not skip a beat. Jesus went forth with a message to influence people to repent and turn to the Kingdom of God (Mt 4:17). Every place he went, synagogue, temple, mountainside, or city street, we find Jesus teaching (influencing) people to change their present way of thinking and to accept God's message. "Jesus did not teach and preach for the sake of teaching and preaching, His purpose was to change persons and conditions..." (Dobbins, *Building Better Churches*, 182). As Jesus brought the earthly portion of His ministry to a close, He told His disciples to go and continue what He had been doing. He did not tell them to go manage the affairs of the Kingdom. He told them to influence people's thinking about Him, to "make disciples" (Mt 28:19).

The Apostle Paul's leadership was one of constant influence, continually motivating people to change their thinking, their lifestyle, their theology. Paul appointed leaders in the churches; he established and trained them to lead their people. Paul's forte was persuasion. He told the Christians in Corinth that his mission was to "try to *persuade* men," (2 Co 5:11). King Agrippa saw what Paul was trying to do as he stood before him to give his testimony, "Do you think that in such a short time you can *persuade* me to be a Christian?" (Ac 26:28).

Paul's letters to the young churches are attempts to influence their thinking. He wrote to the young evangelists,

94

Timothy and Titus, to instruct them as leadership who are able to influence the hearts and minds of people – "As I urged you when I went into Macedonia, stay there in Ephesus so that you may *command* certain men not to teach false doctrines any longer" (1 Ti 1:3). He told Timothy that he would be a good minister of Christ Jesus if he influenced people to follow the Christian lifestyle (1 Ti 4:6, 6:17-18). He told Titus that he was left in Crete to straighten out the situation there and appoint elders (Tit 1:5). This most certainly is a leadership of influence.

Paul encouraged the use of the spiritual gift of leadership by writing, "And in the church God has appointed first of all apostles, second prophets, third teachers . . . also . . . those with gifts of administration. . ." (1 Co 12:28). The Greek word translated "administration" literally means *helmsman*. For a moment, think about the responsibility of the helmsman; is it not to set direction – to influence the ship to go in a chosen direction?

As you look at your responsibilities today, you will find many forces pulling at you to fit various stereotypes formed in the preconceived ideas of people. You must be sure that the model of leadership you choose fits the scriptural pattern.

The Work of Influence

If you have been following the strategy presented in these chapters, you now know your audience and the reality of their situation. From this you have grasped a vision of what you believe the people can accomplish for the Lord. If not, you can be faced with many wonderful ideals of what this ministry can become but of which no one has taken ownership. This becomes a major test of your ability to lead. Their vision may be great, but if there is no ownership it will remain only good ideas – never to be accomplished. Influencing people to see a vision of what they are capable of doing with God's help, to believe in Him and themselves, are the most critical aspects of leadership.

Rules of Influence

Be Willing To Go First

The first rule of influence is that you will never be able to influence and guide others further than you are willing to go yourself. Jesus did not need to be baptized by John, but He did so "to fulfill all righteousness" (Mt 3:15). What He meant was, "I am not going to ask you to do anything I am not willing to do first."

> Leaders must not only have their own commitments, they must move the rest of us toward commitment. They call us to the sacrifices necessary to achieve our goals. They do not ask more than the community can give, but often ask more than it intended to give or thought it possible to give (Gardner, *On Leadership*, 191).

You cannot expect people to give deeper commitment if you are not willing to give it. Famous American naval leader, Fleet Admiral Nimitz, said, "Leadership may be defined as that quality in a leader that inspires sufficient confidence in his subordinates as to be willing to accept his views and carry out his commands"

96

(quoted in Sanders, *Spiritual Leadership*, 35). This *confidence* will only come as the people see their leader in action on their behalf.

The Greek word Paul chooses for leadership is *proistemi* (Ro 12:8; 1 Th 5:12; 1 Ti 3:4, 5, 12; and 5:17). This word is composed of two Greek words and literally translated means *stand before* or *stand first*. People watch to see where their leaders stand, to notice how they walk, to evaluate how they handle life situations. When the people see their leader taking the risk to be out front, then they will follow. "Leadership means that one individual has a better than average sense of what should be done now, and is willing to take the risk to say: 'Let us do this now'"(Greenleaf, *Servant Leadership*, 244).

Leadership Is an Action Word

The second rule of influence is the understanding that leadership is an action word. Direction does not come through words or osmosis. Leadership does not happen just because someone has a position. I have heard ministers berate their church leaders for failing to act. They, however, can never be found outside of their offices – where they arrive late and leave early. Influence will never happen by passing memos and hoping that people will self-start. Gaining a following requires being out among the people actively sharing vision, listening to ideas, overcoming resistance, inspiring change. "Leadership is the process of persuasion or example by which an individual [or leadership team] induces a group to pursue objectives..." (Gardner, *On Leadership*, 1).

Sell the Dream

The third rule of influence is that "the leader is the evangelist for the dream" (Kouzes & Posner, *Leadership Challenge*, 21). A leader must influence people to fulfill the vision, keep the vision in front of them at all times – talk about it, write about it, post it where it can be seen. Continue to deliver the *three-minute vision speech* talked about in chapter one. Be ready to deliver it at any moment.

As the leader, it is your responsibility to influence people's thinking about the vision. This kind of influence can only be exerted if you are totally committed to the vision and constantly keep it in front of the people so they can see where and why they are going and how far they have progressed. I mention once again *The Nehemiah Principle:* repeat the vision every twenty-six days in order to keep people encouraged and going forward.

Influence Vs. Manipulation

The first time I shared my findings concerning *influential leadership* with a group of peers, the response of some was, "That is not leadership; that is manipulation. That is purposely changing people's thinking." Nevertheless, as we have seen in a review of the biblical models, leaders are *thought changers*. When Nehemiah came to the rubble of a city he found a discouraged people. He was able to get them to change their thinking about themselves and their ability to rebuild the wall. He also used his influence on the King of Persia to gather the needed materials for the project. The purpose of the writings of the Apostle Paul was to change the thinking of the leaders who received his letters. If you are to follow in the mold of biblical models then you will have to be a *thought changer.*

Leadership author and teacher, John Maxwell, makes the differentiation between *influence* and *manipulation*, "If I am trying to get someone to do what is best for me, that is *manipulation*. If I am trying to get someone to do what is best for them, that is *influence*" (Maxwell, seminar: *Everything Rises and Falls on Leadership*). Retired US Senator, Mark Hatfield, is quoted, "We should be asking ourselves: are power and leadership things I am using to promote self, career, and prestige? Or are they being used only as a way of serving Christ?" (Myra, *Leaders*, 42) Another Christian author writes, "Like it or not, *power* to influence the behavior of followers is the essential ingredient in leadership" (McKenna, *Power to Follow*, 187). The key is in your ability to convince people to change for their own good, rather than to coerce them to change.

Influence and Authority

There is nothing inherently wrong with desiring to be a leader, as we mentioned earlier in this chapter. Paul urges the Roman Christians to allow a person with the gift of leadership to lead (Ro 12:8). The writer of Hebrews instructs us to "have confidence in your leaders and submit to their authority" (Heb 13:17). The scriptural models do show that it is very possible to be a servant leader and have authority. The Apostle Paul, without shame, defends his authority (2 Co 10:8), yet, at the same time, he notes that the authority he has is for the purpose of building people.

99

As Jesus trained His disciples to be the leaders of the coming Kingdom, He was careful to point out to them that their leadership would have a different focus than the model of leadership in the political and religious world. The current leadership prided itself in its power by "lording over" the people, "exercising authority" (Mt 20:25). This is not the way leadership is to be used in the Kingdom. Instead, Christ-like leadership looks at the needs of people and uses its positional power to provide for those needs (Mt 20:26). The emphasis will not be upon who is the most important, rather, who will use their skills to help people (Mt 20:27). The leadership of the Kingdom is to be a sacrificial leadership, not a power grasping climb for position (Mt 20:28). The Apostle Peter sums up the Kingdom attitude toward authority:

> To the elders. . .Be shepherds of God's flock that is under your care, serving as overseers – not because you must, but because you are willing, as God wants you to be; not greedy for money, but eager to serve; not lording it over those entrusted to you, but being examples to the flock. . . . Young men, in the same way be submissive to those who are older. All of you, clothe yourself with humility toward one another, because, "God opposes the proud but gives grace to the humble."
>
> --1 Peter 5:1-5

The author of the first book to change my concept of leadership claimed that "Leadership is relationship. God is relationship: the relationship of love" (Butt, *Velvet-Covered Brick*, 18). A second author adds, "Leadership is not a title that grants you license to force others to obey; it's a skill you perform, a service you render for the whole group" (Smith, *Learning to Lead*, 15). Christianity teaches a hierarchy in which people carry out different levels of responsibility; nevertheless, there is no difference in the value of each person.

Conclusion

Leader is not a title; it is a responsibility. You only become a leader when you function as one. "All it takes to be a leader is to have somebody follow you. That's all it takes: followers. If people are not following you, you are not a leader. You may have the title, but that's all" (Smith, *Learning to Lead*, 22).

Leadership, therefore, is authoritative, servant-based influence that moves people to follow God's directions. Jesus commissioned his followers to *go make disciples*, which means, *influence life change*. He was an influencer; he expects us to be influencers. We are to influence people to accept His invitation to salvation. And, He expects us to persuade people in our leadership sphere of influence to follow the vision He gives us.

Chapter Seven
Leadership Integrity

Tale of Two Pastors

Pastor Tom began his ministry in a small rural church that had not seen growth in recent years. His first priority was to get to know the people, to listen to their thoughts and needs. From these sessions he carefully gleaned the culture of the congregation and spoke with confidence about a hope for the future. He attended weddings and funerals, even when he was not the officiant. After he had been in the church about six months he led the leadership team through a SWOT Analysis. A vision for the future grew from the study and people were anxious and willing to work to make it happened. During his tenure with that church the congregation nearly doubled in attendance. They began a youth program, a missionary ministry and remodeled the church building. When Pastor Tom was moved to a new location the people cried.

Pastor Ted began his ministry in a strong church in a large city. When he arrived he showed the staff and board a leadership chart in the shape of a wheel with himself at the hub. After his first month he surprised the people with a new worship format that included no music with which they were familiar. In the next two weeks he reassigned staff members and rearranged offices. When he was confronted by the elders of the congregation he boldly reported, "You hired me to be the leader here and I am taking charge." Before completing his first year, Pastor

Ted was fired. When he moved the people breathed a sigh of relief.

Which one of these men was the most powerful – had the most influence on people? I knew both of these men. Pastor Tom was loved wherever he served. People followed him and churches grew strong in the Lord. Pastor Ted walked a rocky road where he never accepted that it was his power-based philosophy that caused his troubles. He claimed that his problems were caused by *unspiritual leaders*.

Power by permission

Power is a frequent discussion in leadership. Books are written about how to attain *power* and how to use it to one's own advantage. Many Christian organizations debate over "who has the power?" However, when all the discussion is done, the purest and greatest power comes from a leader's relationship with the people.

As a leader entering a new ministry you want to be successful. You desire to influence people to fulfill the vision you believe God is giving you. To do that, the principles of scriptural character need to apply. Only then can you expect those principles in the lives of those who follow. There are many excellent authors who have outlined their thoughts around their lists of "what makes a good leader." The bottom line, however, after all the lists have been analyzed, is that leadership will rise or fall on *integrity*. And, *integrity* produces "Power by Permission" – the strongest mode of power known in leadership. This comes as people sense your genuine care linked with your growing reputation for competence. They say, "We trust you; we give you permission to lead us."

Permission through integrity

The need for influential leadership now approaches a fork in the road. When we ask the question, "how to influence?" there begins a separation between modern leadership philosophy and the biblical concept of *servant leadership*. It is possible to go to any bookstore that has a "business section" and find books on how to get your way. The authors are masters of manipulation and power plays. Such secular encouragement could put you in danger of the sin of Diotrephes, "who loved to be first," (3 Jn 9). Secular leadership theory tends to emphasize the organization and the process more than the person. Whereas biblical examples reverse this thinking.

It is important to understand the skills of influence; in fact, these abilities are necessary to Christian leadership. However, when they become an end to themselves they result in leadership practices that are foreign to Scripture. Former U.S. Senator, Mark Hatfield, when asked, "What are the toughest pressures a leader faces?" responded, "The pressures from our own egos" (Hatfield, "Integrity under Pressure," Interview, *Leadership*, Spring 1988, 129)

The Apostle Peter tells us that Christian leaders should not be driven by the same motivations as those of the secular world. Leadership is to be by *example*, (1 Pt 5:1-4). The modern word is *integrity*.

Upon examining the scriptural qualifications for leadership it should be noted that, with the exception of an elder being able to teach (1 Ti 3:2), all other qualities refer to character. Nowhere are there any listings of leadership skills, personality traits or spiritual gifts (Ac 6:1-6, 1 Ti 3:1-7, Tit 1:5-10). "Integrity is foundational for effective leadership; it must be instilled early in a leader's character" (Clinton, *Making of a Leader*, 63).

The word *integrity* is derived from the Latin root word *integer*, which means *undivided* or *whole* (http://dictionary.reference.com/browse/*integer*). A person with integrity is not divided, they are the same person, acting with the same values wherever they are. People with integrity have nothing to hide and nothing to fear. I like the definition of integrity written by leadership author Janet Hagberg,

> Integrity is not a momentary feeling, an act to play. It is a way of being. Integrity is "a quality or state of being of sound moral principle, honest, sincere, upright" . . . This does not mean to be totally perfect, but rather that we care and ask about the difference between right and wrong in dealings with people and organizations and take stands on issues that have been worked out inside. It means not lying, even if we may be served well as a result. It means saying what we genuinely feel and think, not what others want us to feel and think. It means not always having our own way, but being able to compromise when appropriate. It means accepting our whole self and feeling all right about the parts that are not so [pure] accepting being human and imperfect, which may be what it really means

to be complete. It means being worthy of trust and respect even from people who disagree with us (Hagberg, *Real Power: Stages of Personal Power in Organizations*, 149).

Integrity, therefore, is being a complete person, open to those we lead and free to be the person God created us to be. In this freedom, we can work to fulfill God's purpose – freedom to serve simply because we love God and His people. It is having the stability of single-mindedness (Jas 1:8). It is what Jesus called, *pure in heart* (Mt 5:8). It is being wholly devoted to God (Mt 6:22-24). A person of integrity does not try to love God and the world at the same time.

King David in Psalm 15 gives an inspired definition of integrity as he describes who may dwell in God's sanctuary:

> He whose walk is blameless and who does what is righteous, who speaks the truth from his heart and has no slander on his tongue, who does his neighbor no wrong and casts no slur on his fellowman, who despises a vile man but honors those who fear the LORD, who keeps his oath even when it hurts, who lends his money without usury and does not accept a bribe against the innocent. He who does these things will never be shaken (Ps 15:2-5).

Knowing the truth about who we are in Christ is a most important ingredient to integrity. Jesus said, "You will know the truth and the truth will set you free" (Jn 8:32). Paul echoed, "It is for freedom Christ has set us free" (Gal 5:1).

When you are free in Christ, there no longer remains any point to prove, recognition to be gained, or false definitions of success. That freedom will translate to strength and that strength will influence people.

A common misbelief is that a concentration on integrity is *weak*. A. W. Tozier, in his comments on meekness, answers this concern: "The meek man [or person of integrity, *author's insertion*] is not a human mouse afflicted with a sense of his own inferiority. Rather, he may be in his moral life as bold as a lion and as strong as Samson; but he has stopped being fooled about himself (Tozier, *Pursuit of God*, 113)" A major key to integrity is to stop living in a world of misbeliefs about power, position, and wealth – the pseudo-ingredients to success.

The Components of Integrity

As noted earlier, Psalm 15 gives a complete list of the character traits for which God is searching – righteousness, truthfulness, fairness, faithfulness, and generosity. The prophet Micah answers his own question concerning the components of integrity, "And what does the LORD require of you? To act justly and to love mercy and to walk humbly with your God" (Mic 6:8).

At the risk of being presumptuous, allow me to add my findings to the lists noted in Scripture concerning the ingredients of integrity that result in followership.

Respect

When the Apostle Paul decided to give Timothy and Titus a listing of qualifications for those being considered for leadership, he could have summed up his criteria with one word – *respect*. After careful examination his list can be broken into three categories in which a leader must *be above reproach*: in the community ("well thought of by outsiders" 1 Ti 3:7), in the home ("husband of one wife", "manage his own household well" 1 Ti 3:2, submissive children 1 Ti 3:4), and in the church ("able to teach" 1 Ti 3:2, "not a recent convert" and humble 1 Ti 3:6). Over all, in all three areas of life, the leader must have a character that builds respect (temperate, self-controlled, hospitable, not a drunkard, not violent but gentle, not quarrelsome, not a lover of money 1 Ti 3:2-3).

When I speak of *respect* I refer to the trust level built between leader and follower. Respect is gained when followers have assurance that you are a person of integrity and will do what you say. Trust is the foundation to any long-term relationship, in your home as well as in your workplace. Trust results in being given permission to lead.

On September 11, 2001 the entire world watched in horror as highjacked airplanes crashed into the World Trade Center Buildings in New York. The two buildings which took fourteen years to construct crumbled in a matter of minutes. The same is true with respect. It is an indispensable ingredient to integrity that can only be built over time. Its demise, however, can come in seconds with an unthoughtful word, inappropriate action or failure to keep a promise. What started as a beautiful vision and relationship of trust can be destroyed in a heartbeat.

Respect has to be earned. While a student in under-graduate school I used to share my dreams with my professor/mentor. I would give grandiose ideas of my future and ask him how I could attain them. His answer was consistent, "You have to earn the right to do that." In my years in leadership, I have found his words to be prophetic.

Humility

Paul counseled the believers in Rome not to "think of yourself more highly than you ought, but rather think of yourself with sober judgment" (Ro 12:3). He wrote to the Philippian Christians,

> Your attitude should be the same as that of Christ Jesus: Who, being in very nature God, did not consider equality with God something to be grasped, but made himself nothing, taking the very nature of a servant, being made in human likeness. And being found in appearance as a man, he humbled himself and became obedient to death – even death on a cross!
>
> -- Phil 2:5-8

These words were possibly built on Jesus' teaching; "For everyone who exalts himself will be humbled, and he who humbles himself will be exalted" (Lk 14:11). People will willingly follow a leader whose motives they consider to be not self-serving.

Humility is expressed by what we do and say in the presence of other people. It is the willingness to acknowledge another person's presence with a kind word, hand shake, or nod. It is the willingness to listen to a person, offering eye contact and words that show that we under-stand. It is allowing another to speak first and sharing your appreciation for their ideas. It is allowing a member of your staff to excel in their given responsibilities and acknowl-edging their excellence. It is allowing members within the organization to form relationships with other staff members and not being threatened by someone liking them more than us. Above all else, *humility* is giving God credit for your gifts and talents.

Humility is remembering that spiritual gifts and talents come through us but not from us. We have nothing that we have not received from above, and we give all back to God to use (Jn 3:27; 1 Co 4:7).

It has long been my concern that the Christian teachers have given people the wrong sense of humility. Humility has nothing to do with denying your person or abilities. We gain nothing by calling ourselves dust, worms or worthless. The Kingdom is not served by denying that we have any talents or gifts. This teaching is refuted by the scriptures that teach that we do have gifts to be used (Ro 12, 1 Co 12, Eph 4:11-12, 1 Pt 4:10). The Kingdom is served, however, by being good stewards of what Christ died to make us and using God-given abilities for the Kingdom. God is glorified as we give praise and thanks for what He has done and is doing in us and through us.

Confidence

Confidence in what God is doing through you will breed confidence into your people. As they sense assurance, they will follow. "When we esteem our God-given gifts and treat ourselves as persons of worth, we signal, 'I believe God has equipped me to serve by leading. You can put your confidence in me'" (Larson, *Gaining Respect*, 122).

Confidence is the ability to step out on the road of faith and say to those behind, "Follow me." A leader has the assurance to take a risk and if he/she falls, he/she rises to lead again.

Confidence is the ability to pick battles well. It knows when to stand and when to retreat. It is not fretting when someone else wins the battle – because you have a greater picture of the war. It is also being able to recognize what is a battle and what is not. Many people see a crisis in every situation. Confident leaders realize that leadership is a daily experience, and many of today's crises are tomorrow's memories.

Confidentiality

Nothing will kill integrity faster than speaking information you have no permission to share. It is keeping all conversations between you and the person who owns the information – unless that individual releases you to tell others. I have seen pastors ruin their credibility by using a counseling situation in a sermon. I have known of leaders who allowed information about another person to "leak out," thus destroying any trust the people had. The contents of counseling sessions and private conversations are not to be discussed at any time or any way, even with your spouse or another staff member, without permission from the person with whom you spoke. Covey warns:

> One of the most important ways to manifest integrity is to be loyal to those who are not present. In doing so, you build the trust of those who are present" (Covey, *Seven Habits*, 196).

All the time you are telling something that should not be passed on, the person to whom you are speaking is saying, "I will never share anything of importance with you." If that word gets out, you might as well start packing. Without confidentiality, there is no integrity. Without integrity, there is no permission to lead.

Competence

The permission to influence people's thinking can be gained by their observations of us doing our job well. Few people will follow a leader who is sloppy, unorganized, and last minute.

Competence is shown in having answers, or knowing where to find them. Be careful, however, of trying to give quick answers to look good. They have a tendency to haunt you later. There is more integrity in saying, "I will get back to you," than giving a poor answer that causes suspicion concerning your competence.

A question I often receive from young staff members is, "How can I have any influence if I do not have any say in the final decisions? I am just an associate." The answer is simply, "Shine at your desk!" This means to care about those around you and do your job with such competence that people will begin to notice you and seek your opinion. However, be careful of your attitude in doing so. The Apostle Peter tells young leaders who are not pleased with leadership to watch their approach and put their trust in the Lord, casting all their anxieties upon Him – in due time God will lift them up (1 Pe 5:5-7). In the meantime, grow in your competence, shine at your desk.

To maintain competence, you must learn to say "no" to invitations and requests which cannot be fulfilled. People will respect the honesty of a *no* when it is given with good reason. It is better to give quality time to a few responsibilities than to risk a poor reputation. People will follow a leader who knows how to say "no" much further than the person who tries to accomplish everything and, consequently, fails at most.

It is not as easy to build your integrity, to gain the permission to lead once it has been marred. It takes many successes in the eyes of followers to overcome one act of flawed integrity.

Consistency

Since my youth I have heard the saying, "Consistency, thou art a jewel." I have no knowledge of its origin, but I have found it to be a primary ingredient in the recipe for integrity. In leadership, it is the characteristic that treats everyone as equal. It is giving true information to each party as needed. It is taking a stand and maintaining it, unless good reason is presented for rethinking it.

Consistency that leads to integrity grows as you do what you have promised. This is the psalmist's meaning in Psalm 15, a person of spiritual integrity is one "who keeps his oath even when it hurts" (Ps 15:4). A common complaint I hear describes leaders who either forget or find excuses for not following through on promises.

At the very heart of your ability to influence people is your ability to be consistent in word and deed. Followers have a right to know what you are going to do or how you will act in a given situation.

Honesty

Psalm 15 speaks again. A righteous person is one who, "speaks the truth from his heart" (Psalm 15:2). Our subject is how to influence people to fulfill a vision. The ingredient of honesty should be so ingrained in our character that it need not be mentioned. Sadly, even among Christian leaders, that is not a given. Edward R. Murrow, a famous U.S. television news commentator, said, "To be persuasive we must be believable; to be believable, we must be credible; to be credible, we must be truthful" (Kouzes & Posner, *Leadership Challenge*, 25). Honesty is the root of integrity. It is attained when a leader's actions and words constantly affirm each other.

Transparency

Of all the components of integrity transparency is possibly the most difficult. It is the ability to open our heart and mind and allow other people to see inside. The Apostle Paul demonstrates this in the seventh chapter of Romans when he describes his battle with *the flesh*. He does it again in chapters five through eleven of Second Corinthians, as he allows us to see his motives for ministry and his struggles with the elements and people.

As a leader you do not have to hide your weaknesses. On the contrary, when you share your insides, people realize two facts: they are not alone in their battle against temptation and doubt, and they have someone with whom they can share.

There is power in openness. It builds relationships and credibility. It promotes honesty and sharing. It allows a people to bind together by being able to weep together and rejoice together. From here the permission to influence grows.

Conclusion

Think of integrity as a bank account. When you begin your new leadership position, the people will give you a "balance on account" from which you may draw. In the Tale of Two Pastors at the beginning of this chapter, Pastor Tom consistently made *deposits* into his Integrity Account. Whereas Pastor Ted depleted his account within his first weeks and was bankrupt.

In America we have what is called a *honeymoon period* when beginning in a new position. That is the time it takes to use the beginning balance on the account. What is available in the account after the first months depends on whether the leader makes more deposits or withdrawals (unpopular stands, failed attempts or breeches of integrity). It is possible, like Pastor Ted, to be bankrupt in a matter of weeks.

Following the principles of scripture and modeling the components of integrity create deposit to an account. Each deposit will increase influence. Every attempt to manipulate for your own purposes, or break a confidence, or failure in consistency is a withdrawal from that account. If you have not been building your account with true integrity, you will face bankruptcy.

In conclusion: "One thing is sure, no matter what our spiritual and psychological heritage, *it takes time and effort to become a man of Go*d (Getz, *Measure of a Man*, 15)." So it is with influence, you have to earn it. It is a permission to be granted by your followers.

Chapter Eight
Planning for the Future

Introduction

I was invited to lead a workshop at a national pastors' conference on the subject of "Writing a Mission Statement for Your Church." I asked how many of the participants had such a statement. Less than half of the twenty attendees raised their hands. When I asked if they had a plan to fulfill their statement only two raised their hand. When I asked if the plan was in writing, both hands came down. According to British author Samuel Johnson, "The future is purchased by the present" (Dale, *Pastoral Leadership*, 104). The investments you make today will determine how you will spend tomorrow. That is possibly truer in leadership goal setting and planning than in finance. Listen to the findings of one Christian leadership consultant:

> Unfortunately, few congregations have clear long-range plans or even short-range goals. Lacking such strategies, a congregation is likely to be passive. Its activities consist of random procedures that have haphazardly grown up. Its actions are based on vague assumptions or a scattered sense of need rather than on clear objectives. It tends to be programmed more by pressures of the moment than by God-given purpose (Ellis, *Church on Purpose*, 160).

For most new leaders, planning will go against every fiber of their being. It means *time* and most leaders believe time is a commodity to be spent on the present. One pastor told me he wanted to allow room for the Holy Spirit to work. However, my friend told him, "If you think He works without your planning, just think what He would do if you allowed Him to help you plan." The ability of the Holy Spirit to operate within a ministry is directly proportional to the amount of planning leaders are willing to do. All dynamic Christian organizations have at least one characteristic in common: they know where they are going and they have a plan for getting there.

As it was with the *vision* and *scenario*, the goal in planning is *ownership*. The best way to secure ownership is to not short-circuit the process. It does little good for you to approach a governing body and present *your* plan. If they do accept it, they will expect you to fulfill it. You immediately set yourself up for failure. Due to the lack of foundational support you will be unable to do all your plan requires. Subsequently you will be criticized for not following through on what *you* got the leadership council to approve.

When I became the new pastor in an urban church we initially charted eight different groups within the congregation, all working on their own agenda. Instead of cooperation, we had territorial disputes. Instead of fellowship, we had discord. This atmosphere was causing a competitive spirit that had weakened what had been a strong church.

Unless some kind of careful, coordinated planning takes place, a church may even find that each of its groups has mounted its own

120

horse and is riding off in a different direction, literally tearing the church apart (Lindgren, *Foundations*, 228).

A well-run planning process will also pull together the various groups within the organization. It is easy, in the absence of a plan, for departments to view themselves as independent from each other. When they are involved in the planning process, they begin to see how they are a part of the whole.

Many authors have diagramed their understanding of the steps in planning. Although the plans are different, the same principles are present in each. No one is *better* than another. The planning leader needs to adapt the models to fit their leadership style and cultural situation. One item of note, however, is that strategic planning is not a one-time process. It will no sooner be completed when the process will have to begin again. It is this reality that makes planning so distasteful to so many leaders.

A Christian Education Pastor explained his frustration about how his program was progressing. I asked him if he had developed a vision of what his ministry could be and had established a plan to fulfill it. He replied, "Yes, about five years ago, but we have had a complete turnover in staff since then." What he was saying was that he had a vision and plan that were not owned by his present staff.

Beginnings

By now you, as the new leader, have grasped a vision for what your ministry can be. You have built that vision while helping the organization write its mission statement. It has grown as you have studied organizational culture and established a Target Audience. If you are not, as yet, seeing a vision for the future, I would encourage you to take time for a couple of days of spiritual retreat. Sometime you can see better standing on a hill looking down on a city than you can see sitting in the middle of the city. A shared vision is critical for effective strategic planning and implementation. You simply cannot go on without it and lead your people to change and/or to grow.

If you are an associate minister and the larger body does not have a strategic plan, your task will be difficult, but not impossible. Do not jeopardize the growth of your ministry by waiting for them to create a strategic plan. Do, however, discern the climate for such a master plan in the near future. If it is on the horizon, wait. If not, proceed with your people, realizing you might have to make changes and adjustments when a master mission statement and plan are written.

As with Situational Analysis, the planning task force should include a select group of people that represents all the others. The best results are achieved when those who are responsible for accomplishing the objectives have some role in setting them. If you are the Lead Pastor, then you should have staff, board, ministry leaders, and lay people involved. If you are a Youth Pastor, you should have a representation from teens, sponsors, and church leadership.

Compatibility with the Mission Statement

Making a goal compatible with the mission statement should be first. This is a constant point of evaluation throughout the entire planning process. You must bring your leadership team back to the mission statement over and over again. Align every new plan to it, as well as lining it up with Jesus as the Cornerstone. If your goals do not agree with the statement, they must be discarded. Every element of the strategic plan must be in direct support of the mission statement. This sounds simplistic; but, it is not unusual to find goals and mission statements that read like they were created by two different bodies.

Have a copy of the mission statement located in the room where the planning is taking place. Make it large enough for everyone to read. Each goal that is suggested can then be compared with the statement that sets the stage for all planning.

Begin with the Future

The scenario and the specific goals are the pictures of what your people want to accomplish. With that vision in mind, begin to plan backwards – what steps are needed to get there? "It means to know where you're going so that you better understand where you are now and so that the steps you take are always in the right direction" (Covey, *Seven Habits*, 98). *Planning* is simply envisioning what the organization intends to be in the future and setting steps to get there.

Plan to the Present

With the picture of where you want to be in mind (scenario and goals), begin the process of *backdating* to the present. This is the process of setting steps that needs to be accomplished by certain dates to make the vision a reality. Many pre-packaged programs to which a ministry may subscribe (fund-raising campaigns, Vacation Bible Schools, etc.) come with a built in calendar – dates for the committee to be appointed, goals to be selected, letters to be mailed, workers to be trained, calls to be made, etc. A similar calendar can be produced for each goal you wish to achieve. These steps need to be accomplished in order for the future dream to become a reality.

<table>
<tr><td colspan="9" align="center">**May 15th**
Training Seminar</td></tr>
<tr><td>Feb 1</td><td>Feb 15</td><td>Mar 1</td><td>Mar 15</td><td>Apr1</td><td>Apr 15</td><td>May 1</td><td>May 15</td></tr>
<tr><td>Planning Meeting</td><td>Poster Info</td><td>Poster Design</td><td>Printer</td><td>Mailing Preparation</td><td>Mail</td><td>Publicity Follow up</td><td>Seminar*</td></tr>
<tr><td colspan="8">*A line similar to this must be developed for each responsibility for the May 15th seminar.</td></tr>
</table>

The importance of each step in the backdating process is threefold. The first is *accountability,* which is essential to everything. There has to be time for people to accomplish their assigned task for the whole to be realized. However, people need to know when they are expected to have completed their responsibility.

The second reason for this backdated timeline is *communication.* You will not be long in leadership before you are frustrated with seminar and conference flyers that arrive in the mail three days before the event. Often they will arrive on Wednesday asking you to publicize Friday's *important event* in your weekly newsletter that was mailed Tuesday. If a timeline is not set, communications become a last minute dash that could subvert hours of planning.

The third reason for this backdated time line is *prayer*. As each step of the plan unfolds, you and your leadership will be able to pray specifically for each need. It is also possible to keep your prayer warriors abreast of these needs. I am sure you will agree that prayer is the key to fulfilling chosen objectives.

Planning for the Future

In this book I have spent much time outlining the need and the ways to research your membership, as well as the community. I have also encouraged you to lead your leadership in a *Situational Analysis* of your present situation. These are needed for understanding and goal setting; however, herein lies the danger. Members of your leadership team who have a larger *rear-view mirror* than front *window* will want to go back and plan for the past.

I faced this in my first ministry in a small rural Midwest town. When the decision was being made to remodel the eighty-five-year-old building, there was no thought for a nursery. Members had neglected the fact that the town was slowly becoming a bedroom community for a nearby city. When the vision called for the creation of a nursery, some members said, "Our people are older, we have no need for a nursery." When it was pointed out that young couples were moving to town they responded, "When I brought my children, they sat on my lap during worship." Therefore, original remodeling plans were drawn up without a nursery facility.

At that time I was twenty-three years old and we had our first child whom my wife was holding during each service. After some time had elapsed in the planning process, I asked leaders, "Do you ever want young couples to attend this church? We have a vision for reaching young adults; if we are going to do that we need to plan for them." The Building Committee listened and the project was completed with a new nursery. The people were pleased when young families began coming.

Goal Setting

Before Nehemiah was sent to rebuild the walls of Jerusalem, the king inquired, "What is it you need?" (2:4 – author's paraphrase) and "How long will it take you?" (2:6 – author's paraphrase). The King wanted a better under-standing of Nehemiah's project; therefore, he questioned him concerning his goals. These are two excellent questions for your next step in the strategic planning process. Because he had spent three to five months studying the project, Nehemiah was able to lay his plan and requests before the king.

Now that your planning group is ready and the dates for the meeting scheduled, go back to the scenario you created in the *Situational Analysis* meetings. That scenario is a dream to motivate people to see what can happen. The next step is to put feet on the dream and make it a reality. This begins with defining your mission and setting the goals; and it ends with the celebration of their reality.

Make the Goals Accomplishable

The first criterion of a good goal is to make sure it can be accomplished within a reasonable amount of time. It would be unrealistic for most Christian organizations to say, "We will double participation in two months" – unless you are beginning with some very small numbers. To set a goal that can never be reached will only breed discontent and a sense of failure. It is better to accomplish small goals once a month, than never to attain a major goal in two years. There is also the problem of setting long-range goals without measurable increments. Without smaller goals and measurement dates, there is no celebration and the people lose interest. Then you, as the leader, are the one criticized for failing to do what was promised.

A real tension arises at this point. What is the line between faith goals and real goals? I was once challenged by a statement attributed to John Haggai, "Try something so impossible that if God is not in it, it is destined to fail." Even faith-stretching goals must be kept in the realm of measureable reality. I do believe God can do the impossible. I have seen God do the impossible. However, the goals that drive people day by day will be those that give a sense of accomplishment. Perhaps, a series of small goals will lead to the major, faith-stretching goal that only God can accomplish. This brings us to the second criterion for goal setting.

Make Your Goals Measurable

Goals that have clear points of attainment give people the opportunity to celebrate and build confidence. This is the quantitative aspect of goal setting. Every goal needs have a date, number, or some means of measuring completion. Without a means of measuring goals, there will be no sense of growth or maturity.

In a questionnaire I use during premarital counseling, I ask the couple to write out "their goals for their marriage." Nine times out of ten they say, "We want to live long and be happy." My questions to them are, "How long is long?" and "How will you know you are happy?" A frequent response is, "We will have children, a house of our own, and a good retirement." I love to come back with, "How many children, how big of a house, and by when?" I can usually count on some sort of display of frustration at this time. However, let me ask, "How can we celebrate success if success is never defined?"

Many ministries have a dream, but no plan. I have never consulted with a Christian organization that did not have the dream *to grow*. When I press for measurable definitions of that dream, I usually receive the same signs of frustrations I get from the young couples. This type of goal setting is not easy because it creates the possibility of failure. There is a fear in saying "We will grow twenty per cent by the last Sunday in December." What if it is not accomplished? It is much easier to simply say, "We plan to grow this year." There is, however, no stretch, no excitement generated, and no cause for celebration.

Make Your Goals Flexible

I have a favorite example I like to use to illustrate the need for flexible goal setting. A nearby church became serious about adopting a five-year plan. They hired a consultant who took them through the steps and they produced a very impressive plan. Their five year plan called for the purchase of a new church van in the fifth year. About three months after completing the planning process, a woman in the congregation donated the entire amount needed to purchase the new van. The "Five Year Plan," however, called for the purchase in the fifth year. The leadership, therefore, voted to put the money in the bank until it was *time*. That is inflexibility!

One of my seminary professors told the story of an American football coach who told his team leader to run two plays and then kick the ball away. The first play went half the distance to the goal. The second play put the ball inches from scoring. However, according to plan, on the third play the team leader kicked the ball to the other team.

> This illustrates for us the importance of leadership in Christian organizations. An action plan is viable only for as long as the assumptions that called for it are valid. Some Christian organizations, I fear, operate on the basis of pray, plan, and [kick]! Once the operation has been committed to God in prayer, the plans are fortified by the assurance that they are "the will of God," and regardless of signs and evidences to the contrary, the execution of the plan will relentlessly take place (Anderson, *Minding God's Business*, 83).

Flexibility is the necessary watchword.

Conclusion

I have a beautiful picture in my office that I took on a hiking trip. It shows an inviting path leading into a forest. However, it does not show anything about what lies at the end of the trail. It depicts the many ministries that look good on the outside, but in reality, are not headed to any particular destination.

It is impossible to achieve goals if you do not have any. Sometimes this idea is so simple that people overlook it. With no planning they waste time and energy just wandering. Not to plan is actually a plan in itself and it is a slow path to nowhere.

The purpose of this book is to help you create a strategy for leadership as you begin your ministry. Without a plan there is no strategy and all the work you have done to date will slip away to the tune of "Well, there's another leader who made promises they never delivered."

In his 1993 "State of the State Address," Peter Wilson, at that time the Governor of California, said, "We either shape the future, or we suffer it."

Chapter Nine
When the Future Means Change

Introduction

I served five churches in my thirty-four years as a pastor. Four of those five churches were in a state of decline (the other was a new church plant). Therefore, every situation into which I was called was one requiring major changes if the church was to survive. Some of what I know about making changes comes from study, some from sharing experiences with friends, but mostly from my own mistakes.

Leading change will be one of the most difficult times in your leadership experience. You have done your demographics and culture homework. You see all the needs and potentials. Therefore, drawing upon everything you have learned in your training, programs observed in other like organizations, and your own ideals, you set out to make major changes for a healthy future. You believe that these changes are sure to "make this ministry what it ought to be." This is often where the reality of the difficulties in working with people becomes a major hindrance to a leader's joy. These troubles are unnecessary. There are steps that can be taken to lead people in change, and understanding them can save you as a leader and keep you happy and fulfilled for many years in the vocation of your calling.

"Earn the right," as I coach leaders today, I constantly remind them of this. Everything within your training is telling you that there are jobs to be done, changes to be made, exciting new programs to be launched. You are a leader and

131

leaders take people to new places. Leaders are pioneers and pioneers face difficulties. Your role is to help people stay encouraged and navigate new territory. But first, you must earn the right to suggest a new direction through your integrity, relationships and competence.

Some people will not be as anxious to make changes as you are. All around you will be people who will discourage idealism. When I met the man whom I followed in my first church, he told me that his philosophy of ministry was, "If you don't kick a sleeping dog he won't bite you." An elder in that church continually told me, "When you have been around as long as I have, you won't get as excited about these things." A young associate pastor in another church was told by his Lead Pastor, "I am not going to disturb what is happening here and make people unhappy; I want to retire here." (Later, this Lead Pastor was forced to leave this church because the people wanted the church to grow.)

"There are only three kinds of people in the world – those that are immovable, those that are movable, and those who move them!" (Ford, *Transforming Leadership*, 91) You will meet all three. Your job will be to discover which is which, and then train the movers, move the movable and love the immovable. An important principle to grasp, however, is that some of the *immovable* are the well-meaning people. They truly believe that their stand is best for the people. There is no need to fight them. Listen to them, get to know them, their story and love them. Some of my immovable people actually became change agents for what was good and positive. You would do well to understand this principle and these people.

132

It is risky to propose changes within any organization, especially a body which has had its culture set for many years. After a long period of time of handling affairs the same way, a group becomes like an airplane that once it is in the air is switched to *automatic pilot* and flies itself. They are coasting and failing to fulfill their mission. It is the leader's responsibility to prevent the plane from going down. What people don't realize is that change is going to take place one way or another. Either the plane is going to crash, killing everyone on board, or it is going to land, re-fuel, and continue to function according to its design.

In 1532, Machiavelli wrote in his classic book, *The Prince*, "There is nothing more difficult to carry out, or more doubtful of success, or more dangerous to handle than to initiate a new order" (Machiavelli, The Prince, no date). What causes a person to fear change? How can you successfully help people overcome the fear of change? Let's address these questions.

A Critical Issue to Understand

As you begin a new leadership assignment it is critical that you understand that there are few people more loved than the former leader. Even if s/he was a scoundrel, you will find people who loved them. Their leaving has produced a major change. There is insecurity about your coming. What you will be experiencing is known as *termination emotions*. Leading people through this time will be your first opportunity to lead them through *change*.

Studies reveal that an organization goes through similar stages of *grief* as the person who has just lost a loved one. For you to insensitively walk into a new responsibility and begin to change everything former leaders have done would be like going to the home of a grieving widower and rearranging the living room furniture the week after his wife died. To speak against a past leader would be tantamount to slandering a deceased family member.

One of the first and most effective *ministries* you can perform is to help the people through this period. Allow them to talk about their departed leader. Listen to the same stories over and over. Do not be threatened by references to their name. Realize that some people will need to work through the grief caused by a leader's exit. An expert on transitions writes,

> It's important that you neither seek to stifle the expression of these feelings, nor that you feel that parishioners are comparing you to their former pastor. They are simply trying to gain resolution to some powerful feelings so they can get on with their relationship with you (Oswald, *New Beginnings*, 11).

Even if the former leader was asked to leave, there will be *Termination Emotions* to work through. You may have to deal with what is called, *inherited debt* (Oswald, *Pastor as Newcomer*, 8) – if the former leader was guilty of moral failure, lying, apostasy, or laziness, you will be watched with a careful eye to see if you are guilty of the same. You will need to be sensitive to their feelings and allow them this caution. Your understanding will go much further than your anger. How you handle *Termination Emotions* will have a great bearing on your ability to lead in change.

Steps to Introducing Change

As you patiently help people work through transition you gain *deposits* into your Leadership Account. But, now the question arises, "How to bring about the needed changes uncovered in the Situational Analysis?" I like the analogy of making a candle. First you have to melt the wax, then mold it, and then allow it to harden (Griffin, *Mind Changers*, 5). Careful adherence to these guidelines will help you bring about purposeful and organized changes. Failure to follow them can result in discouragement.

Melt

When we started talking about a much needed remodel of the Anaheim church building, I was surprised when one of the leading dissenters was a young entrepreneurial leader in our church and community. His resistance did not make sense to me until I sat with him and he told me about the emotional attachment he had to the building. He had grown up attending church in that building, his wedding ceremony was there and family members' funerals were there. He was afraid that if the building was given major changes he would lose all those memories (Termination Emotions). I was able to share with him our vision for a better facility and share how what would be gained would be better than what he perceived would be lost.

When an organization's culture has been frozen over a period of time, it becomes necessary to slowly melt that culture to bring the needed change. This is where the risk of change becomes reality. Most people are uncomfortable with change and will either fight against it or ignore it. Griffin notes, "Wax cannot be molded when it's hard. It has to be melted first. So do people" (Griffin, *Mind Changers*, 5). This is a slow and loving process of breaking down the old ways, so the new can be introduced. Help people recognize that some past ways of organizational thinking, feeling, and doing are no longer effective.

The key to melting the present situation is to help people understand they can come through the change safely and that the new way will be good for everyone. That is why it is so important to go into a change situation with your homework done. You have studied the culture and the demographics. This should give you a strong understanding of what forces you will face. Before proceeding, however, if you have not found the answers to the following questions, ask them of people whose knowledge you can trust:

1. How have major changes been accepted in the past?

2. Did these changes take a long time?

3. Were changes made in spite of opposition, or did a few negative votes stop the process?

4. Would you consider this organization to be flexible and resilient?

With this knowledge, and having spent time revealing your integrity, you are now ready to begin the melting process. With the facts and permission to lead, you can say to your people, "We have a problem here, but we can solve it."

At this point let me again mention the importance of listening. To forge ahead without hearing your people is suicide. *Active listening* is the first step after sharing the vision. If you want to melt people's resistance, hear their fears. Meet with them, listen to them and pray with them. Nehemiah remained available to his people to hear their fears and address them (Neh 4:12-14). However, as you read Nehemiah's narrative, notice how often he prayed. To be an agent of change, be a person who will listen, respond, affirm, explain and pray.

When James led the Council at Jerusalem concerning the entrance of Gentiles into the Kingdom (Acts 15:4-12) – a major change – he began the meeting by listening to what everyone had to say – first, the Pharisees spoke (15:5), then Peter (15:7), followed by Paul and Barnabas (15:12). It was only after hearing all sides that James spoke (15:13). A leader who desires to melt the present situation must have an open ear. People must feel you are safe to approach and that they will be heard.

Presenting the Idea of Change

The grid on the following page explains two ways of initiating change; two ways to *melt* a situation and lead your people to a new direction.

Directive Change

The first, *directive change,* is the *fast melt* of *authority; i.e.* "this is the way it will be done." This might be easily accomplished in a business where the leader can

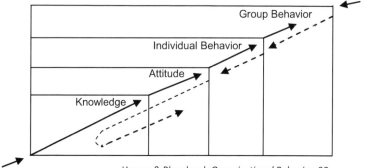

threaten followers with the loss of their job or reduction in salary. However, in an organization where you are working with volunteers in a long ingrained culture, this does not work. In fact, it is next to impossible unless you are a leader who has spent years of making deposits into your integrity account; or you are leading in a culture that gives the leader absolute authority. Even in the latter situation, I do not recommend *directive change*.

Participative Change

Participative change, the second way to melt the present is more ideal if you want the people to own it and create a new culture. This method recognizes that change is a process of teaching, explanation, and discussion. It is designed to help the people begin to see the good the change can make. After they understand (gain knowledge of) the principles and reasons for the new direction, the change becomes a part of their thinking (attitude) and their behavior. As more individuals accept the new thinking, the group behavior will adjust. Change is a process of working through all the ideas, fears, facts, and planning for the new direction.

When the process is ignored, there is a price to pay. When change is brought about quickly, through a *fast melt*, people's performance might be different; their hearts and minds (as noted by the dashed line on the chart), however, must still go through knowledge and attitude adjustment before the new direction is accepted. *Participative change*, on the other hand, takes people through these levels as decisions are made (Hersey and Blanchard, *Organizational Behavior*, 343).

The way you introduce change is every bit as important as the change itself, and it may be the determining factor in whether your vision will succeed. People will make changes if they see the purpose and know that everyone will come out winners.

Mold

After you have earned the right to speak, have presented the facts, and the people are ready to make the change, it is now necessary to lead them in bringing together the plan. Notice, I did not say, "present them with your plan." If you do, as mentioned in a former chapter, they are most likely to agree and leave you to do it. If you want to go into the next step of change and have your people participate, lead them in the solution or present a shared solution developed with trusted leaders. The goal is to influence *ownership*. Here are four keys to molding the change in a way that helps people say, "We want this."

139

Honor the Past

One of the most important lessons in the whole subject of the dynamics of change is to *honor the past*. One leadership author writes, "The most important point I want to make is that those who are trying to create a new organizational future must also honor the past" (Wilkens, *Corporate Character*, xi).

Remember Pastor Ted in chapter seven? Within the first month of his leadership he made major culture-changing decisions without permission. He stood before the people and announced, "Now we are going to do it right." What the people heard was, "All your past and present leadership has been wrong. We are throwing out everything they have done and begin to do it right." This infuriated people, especially those who loved the former leaders. An author who is considered an expert in bringing change writes,

> In conceiving of a different future, change masters have to be historians as well. When innovators begin to define a project by reviewing the issues with people across areas, they are not only seeing what is possible, they may be learning more about the past; and one of the prime uses of the past is in the construction of a story that makes the future seem to grow naturally out of it in terms compatible with the organization's culture (Kanter, *Change Masters*, 283).

The point is not to cling to the past, but to build on it. When people put up resistance to change it is usually because they feel they are going to lose everything they hold dear (Transition Emotions). Knowing the culture will help you know priorities, and being a change agent you can use these values to build a new culture. This is where most people lose their jobs. A study conducted in America found that five out of every seven new executives who lost their jobs within the first year did so because they tried to make changes that did not honor the past (Wilkens, *Corporate Character*, 15). The following is a list of guidelines to help you "honor the past":

1. Look for what was good in the past and build on it.

2 .Identify the principles in past decisions that will be principles in this change.

3. Speak highly of the people who promoted and followed through on the decisions that are being changed.

4. Find current examples of success.

5. Where possible, use some of the past in the new.

6. Label eras – picture organizational history as being divided into eras.

7. Remember *Transitional Emotions* and mourn the loss of a cherished past.

People are always going to remember the past; our job is to help them to build on whatever is true, noble, right, pure, lovely, admirable and praiseworthy (See Phil 4:8).

The prophet Samuel had the Israelites set up a stone monument and named it *Ebenezer* to help the people remember God's deliverance (1 Sa 7:12). If you are introducing major change, you might want to think of some type of *Ebenezer* – a plaque, a painting, etc. Former Israeli Foreign Minister, Shimon Peres, said, "In difficult times people choose to remember rather than think" (Shimon Peres, CBS, Aug. 30, 1993). It is our job to help them remember God's faithfulness in both the good and the bad times and that faithfulness will take us through this change also.

The degree to which you need to honor the past will be determined by how dramatic the change is in the eyes of the people. There are two levels of change – simple and major. You need to correctly discern how your proposed change will impact your people.

Simple Change

When I first arrived at a new location of service I usually rearranged the office so that it fit me and my style of working. Although some people noticed, few people cared about this change. There were times when we would rearrange the order of worship – few people notice. These are fairly insignificant changes in the minds of most people and can be done with little explanation or process. These are *simple* changes that do not disrupt the culture.

Major Change

When I became the Lead Pastor in Anaheim, the church building had two large three-sided pulpits, one on each side of the stage. We affectionately referred to them as *the chariots* because their construction reminded us of pictures we had seen of the ancient vehicles. The former pastors had always preached from the pulpit on the left; however, I was never comfortable speaking from behind any pulpit. To move away from the pulpit would be a major cultural shift in this 100 year old congregation. In my mind it was a *simple* change, but I had learned enough from my initial visits with people that such a move would be seen as a *major* shift of tradition.

I first learned the purpose for two pulpits (one for preaching and the other for reading Scripture). Then I visited some of the older church members where I remarked on the beauty of the pulpits, but explained my discomfort as I felt any pulpit was a barrier between me and the people. They asked a couple of questions, told me a couple of *pulpit stories,* and then decided that as long as I used the pulpits for funerals, the change would be alright. On my first Sunday to preach outside the pulpit I shared appreciation for the beauty of the pair and gave my reason for stepping away. I only know of one person who commented to one of the families I had called on and that family told them, "It's alright; he talked to us about it."

Later, when we remodeled the church building the architect suggested the removal of both pulpits to make the stage area more usable. The older people said, "We must have a pulpit." The problem was solved with a clear plastic one that solved their need for this piece of furniture and my feelings of it being a barrier.

Major changes are radical in the minds of the recipients. They are a shift in an accepted practice. Because they present an entirely new order, they create the need for greater preparation, teaching, and time involvement. The greater the change, the greater the risk and the more the resistance.

The natural reaction to problems requiring a *major change* is to solve it by pouring in more resources of what worked in the past – make more or make it bigger. (If you do not like preaching from a pulpit on the side of the stage, build a third one in the middle.) One historical example describes the British army during the American Revolution. They had always won battles by having superior fire power, lining troops in rows across the battlefield and marching at the enemy. "What do you do, however, with American militia who hide behind rocks and trees?" The British solution was to call for more troops from England (Anderson, R. "Theology of Change," class notes). When a leader suggests that traditional worship is not bringing in new families, the reaction is, "It worked for my generation." The suggested solution, "Sing the hymns louder," maybe with a Praise Team. Leith Anderson notes, "When the institution faces threats, the most common response is retrenchment and defensiveness, and resistance to change is strengthened" (Anderson, L. *Dying for a Change*, 112). Your job as leader is to lead to new solutions that honor the past, but build for the future.

Major change is never easy. Nevertheless, with proper preparation and communication the organization can be molded into a new way of fulfilling its mission. However, the step to molding a change is a repeated warning.

144

Make it Contextual

At the risk of being dangerously repetitive, allow me to repeat this word of caution. A very common mistake leaders are making in Christian organizations is the desire to bring a successful program from another culture to their own.

> "A myth among many executives is that they can implement the practices of successful companies and reap their success...You cannot copy execution; you have to develop it through trial and error with motivated [people] (Wilkens, *Corporate Character*, 10-11).

Each situation is unique and any change must be designed within its context., Every organization must go through its own process of self-evaluation and decide on its own program for change. Christian research specialist, George Barna writes, "Ministry by mimicry almost invariably results in deterioration, rather than growth" (Barna, *User Friendly Churches*, 16). If you find a successful program, bring it through the proper steps to make it fit into your culture. Then instead of saying, "We are adopting a successful program," you can lead your people to exclaim, "This is new. This is us. This is exciting. This is what we will gain." It becomes their idea.

Make Hard

"A new belief is like hot wax – it can't support itself until it becomes firm" (Griffin, *Mind Changers*, 8). The change is not complete until people have totally accepted it (ownership) and it becomes a part of their thinking and habit. The leader's challenge is not only to get people to make a change, but to get them to accept it and begin to tell others of their pride in it – they *own* the new change. You will know you have accomplished this when people walk away and tell others, "This is what _we_ planned," or "This is how _we_ do it." When a person owns the new culture, his/her participation in it will be a joy.

This hardening stage can be carefully brought about through praise and optimistic reporting. When people begin to function in the change, let them know that they are appreciated. When someone excels, let all the people know your appreciation and how the new order has benefitted them. When the new vision produces results, tell as many people as possible. The more positive feedback, the harder the new change sets.

Conclusion

I once announced a major change to our leaders through a letter which arrived four days before their regular meeting. I told them I was going to propose "a radical new change" for them to consider. I proceeded to outline what I wanted them to be thinking about. I hit them cold with *major change*. Before I got to the meeting I knew my proposal was in trouble. They were already discussing "the letter" in private conversations. I had overwhelmed them with my proposal. Needless to say, I came away from the meeting with a unanimous rejection of my "great idea."

During that ill-fated meeting, I realized what I had done. I began to backtrack. Keeping the same ideas for future direction, I began to present them in small simple bits at meetings and in private conversation. After a period of

146

time, they were bringing up the new concepts during the meetings as if they were their own. They made some *major changes* in church planning that had a vast impact on the future of the congregation.

A major reason new leaders are quickly discouraged with their calling has its roots in the dynamics of change. New leaders often take a grand new idea to the leadership and present it in one huge chunk. They usually do so with great excitement. Then, when the idea is rebuffed, they feel personally rejected. It only takes a couple such experiences before they begin to think of a career change.

With change, "slow is fast." Effective leaders do not create massive changes all at once. They have a clear idea of where they are headed and keep the end in focus. They are patient, always listening, always teaching, always testing the direction of the change. One author likens the proper change process to an automobile engine that operates by a series of explosions. Any one of the explosions, if outside the engine chamber, could be devastating. However, if they are kept small, controlled, and inside the chamber, the automobile becomes a useful vehicle (Muck, *When To Take a Risk*. 127). The same principle is true of change. If we keep the explosions small, simple and controlled the vehicle will take us forward.

Be patient with your people in this change process. Think of it as a child learning to walk. The child tries, fails, has partial success, learns, bumps its nose, cries, and tries again. It has many failures before it succeeds. However, in the end, walking is worth all the risks to learn.

147

In his inaugural address, U.S. President John F. Kennedy said,

> All this will not be finished in the first one hundred days. Nor will it be finished in the first one thousand days, nor in the life of this administration, not even perhaps in our lifetime on this planet. But let us begin (Kennedy, Jan 20, 1961).

SECTION 3

Third Leadership
Responsibility

EMPOWERING TO ACCOMPLISH

Chapter Ten
The Power Of Empowerment

Introduction

If you have been following the guidelines of this book, you now understand the makeup of your organization and your community. You have done an analysis of the Strengths, Weaknesses, Opportunities, and Threats that are present. You have dreamed with your leaders and have influenced them to follow through on that dream. Now you come to the most critical part of your leadership, giving them the tools they need to make the vision a reality.

You are now getting to know your people as individuals with their unique stories and abilities. If you have followed this strategy closely you have invested more than a year with them. If you are to continue forward as a leader, you need to begin to teach your people "how" to fulfill the dream and encourage them every step of the way. A Chinese Proverb says,

If you want one year of prosperity, grow grain.

If you want ten years of prosperity, grow trees.

If you want one hundred years of prosperity, grow people (Kouzes & Posner, *Leadership Challenge*, 161).

151

Another author gives the following test of your leadership success, "Do those served grow as persons? Do they, while being served, become healthier, wiser, freer, more autonomous?" (Greenleaf, *Servant Leadership*, 13)

The development of people into skilled workers and leaders is the most important task you will undertake outside of proclaiming the gospel.

> The measure of leadership is not the quality of the head, but the tone of the body. The signs of outstanding leadership appear primarily among the followers. Are the followers reaching their potential? Are they learning? Striving? Do they achieve the required results? Do they change with grace? (DePree, *Leadership Is an Art*, 10).

Jesus

Jesus invested three years teaching and modeling the Kingdom message to twelve men. With their education completed and their understanding of His deity assured, Jesus' disciples were empowered to accomplish the task for which they were chosen. Jesus' last official earthly act was to commission them to do what they had been taught (Matthew 28:19). He had already promised the Holy Spirit to be their helper in accomplishing the task (John 14:16).

These twelve men were to fulfill the vision of the Kingdom. They were to influence people to become disciples and, thus, change their lives and priorities. Now Jesus commissions them to empower the new believers with the same teachings He had given them.

Empowerment is the third leadership responsibility that cannot be delegated to anyone else. The true test of leadership skills is seen in those trained and freed to fulfill the purpose. Therefore, as we enter into the final phase of developing a strategy for leading a new ministry, I would like to share a plan for empowering others to accomplish the vision you have influenced them to own. This plan begins with how you see yourself as a leader.

The Player-Coach

A Team Builder

There are many different philosophies of leadership; however, few fit the biblical principles. The leader as a *player-coach* approaches the biblical model to help implement vision, influence, and empowerment. The *player-coach* not only teaches and oversees the team, he takes his place on the playing field to add his gifts to the goals of the team.

The great Old Testament leaders such as Moses, David and Nehemiah are examples; they not only gave leadership, they also participated with the people in its accomplishment. It was not a philosophy of telling people what to do; it was one of let's-do-this-together.

Jesus was a player-coach. Besides actively ministering to the needs of people, He focused on training leaders to continue the vision of the Kingdom. In Paul's letters to Timothy and Titus, a coach gives his young *players*

153

directions and pep talks. Therefore, I want to encourage you to think of yourself as a *player-coach*. I was first challenged to this thinking about leadership when Elton Trueblood delivered a lectureship at the seminary I attended. In his book he writes,

> Since the equipping minister must not be above the heat of battle, he is, ideally, not only a coach, but a "playing coach," sometimes carrying the ball himself and sometimes seeing to it that another carries it. Thus, he is both a minister and the encourager, a teacher and a developer of his fellow ministers, who are the members of the Church of Christ (Trueblood, *Incendiary Fellowship*, 43-44).

There is such a joy to be found in teaching principles and watching people grow. I love to see men and women develop to their potential and become leaders in their own right. "The glory of the coach is that of being the discoverer, the developer, and the trainer of the powers of other men (Trueblood, *Incendiary Fellowship*, 43)."

> Coaching involves the on-the-job, day-by-day spending of time with your people, talking with them about your game strategies, providing them feedback about their efforts and performance. And when the game is over, you get together with the players and analyze the results of your efforts. . .And then it's practice and getting ready for the next game (Kouzes & Posner, *Leadership Challenge*, 257).

A Participant

Many sports teams have multiple coaches. In American football, there are coaches who sit high above the field and watch the game through binoculars and send instructions through a telephone. They don't get involved with the players; they don't hear the sounds or smell the sweat. They are merely masters of strategy. Like these non-interactive coaches, you will hear those who adopt a corporate style of leading. They operate as a CEO – aloof from the people. This does not work with the biblical model of leadership. Moses took his part in hearing the needs of his people (Ex 18:13-16). David rode into battle beside his men. Nehemiah worked with a trowel in one hand and sword in the other. Until we do as Jesus did in the *Incarnation* and "'pitch our tent" among our people (Jn 1:14) and become one with them, the task will not be completed. "You cannot paint a shepherd by himself - you will always find him with his sheep" (Hian, *Making of a Leader*, 31). This is true for the coach also – he exists for the team, the team does not exist for the coach.

A Builder of People

The purpose of the playing coach described earlier is *empowerment* – the ability to teach, give responsibility, and remove obstacles blocking a follower's way to success. This goes beyond the important task of mentoring; this means releasing and trusting them for a specific task.

As a coach, use your power and position to enable your people to fulfill the vision you have helped them build. This will involve Paul's directions to use scripture for "teaching, reproof, correction, and training in righteousness" (2 Ti 3:16). All of these are the tasks of the coach.

This brings us to an important principle – "people will rise to the level of their leader's expectation." When our daughter was in junior high we proudly attended a concert in which seven school choirs participated. All the choirs came from similar sized schools in the same district. Every choir was led by a college-trained Music teacher. However, the performances of the individual choirs were as different as night and day. Three of the seven choirs were very small. The audience could hardly hear them as they sang with little emotion or movement. The other four choirs were large, full of energy and smiles as they sang loudly and moved with synchronized choreography. The observation was that each choir sang to the level of the expectations of its leader.

Leading is coaching and coaches pour their knowledge into the players to make them the best they can possibly be. The coach's effect can be felt throughout the organization. The coach sees how a situation can best be met and begins to set the strategy and training to meet it. They make players feel important because they are involved in the mission. As a coach you become the head cheerleader. You need to be the first to recognize and reward achievement.

Because of empowerment, big problems seem smaller and big challenges seem easier. Responsibilities cease to be a task. And, as Hebrews 13:7 suggest leadership begins to take on a new dimension of joy.

The Ministry of Empowerment

Seeing Potential

The *priesthood of all believers* (1 Peter 2:9) is a popular topic. It teaches that everyone should use their spiritual gifts in ministry to others (1 Peter 4:10). However, many ministries remain full of people who do not know how to use those gifts. They are told the problems, challenged to get involved, but never taught how. "To succeed at leadership you *must* be a teacher of people" (Bennis, *Why Leaders Can't Lead*, 155). The priesthood of all believers is a great idea when it is practiced, people need to be helped and encouraged to use what God has built into them. A good coach will "watch for underdeveloped powers, to draw them out, to bring potency to actuality in human lives." (Trueblood, *Incendiary Fellowship*, 41).

Empowerment is the ability to be able to see people and their skills for where they can best serve the Kingdom. Bo Jackson was a famous American football player. He was one of the finest offensive players of his time. However, in high school he played defense. When Jackson attended the university the coach watched him and told him he could better serve the team by playing offense. His high school coach never saw him as a runner. A coach sees potential in people and is willing to reassign responsibility so that potential can be actualized. It is this reason that, in the next chapter, I would like to share some thoughts on how to understand where a person can best serve on the team.

Challenging Potential

When Jesus first saw Andrew's brother, Simon, He saw in him a potential for leadership. Therefore, instead of addressing him by his given name, He called him *Peter*, meaning "The Rock" (Jn 1:42). Three years later, Peter was a defeated disciple. He felt that since he had betrayed Jesus there was no longer any place for him in the work of the Kingdom. Jesus met him on the seashore and refocused his attention on the task for which he had been trained (Jn 21:15-21). Jesus saw Peter's potential, challenged him to live up to it and restored him when he had failed. Peter went on to become a dynamic leader in the Kingdom of God.

Empowering people to function in ministry means to challenge them and stretch them to reach their potential. It is the leader's responsibility to "raise the bar gradually and offer coaching and training to build skills to get over each new level" (Kouzes & Posner, *Leadership Challenge*, 61).

One of the defining moments of my life was when an elder in my home church came to me when I was fourteen years old and said, "You need to be a preacher; and I will help in any way to see that happen." Later, my pastor came to me and said, "I would like for you to be a part of the youth preaching team; and I will train you."

A leader is always on the lookout for potential. If we believe what scripture says, we all have abilities to use in the Kingdom of God (1 Pt 4:10). Many people just need the encouragement of a leader to recognize and accept what God has built in them. After you have challenged them, offer opportunities for learning, spend time with emerging leaders and encourage them to reach their ability.

The Goal of Empowerment

A Peace in Your Own Absence

A leader strives to bring out the best in people. Pray, sweat, teach, and encourage. You will know that maturity is growing when three goals begin to be seen. First, when you can walk away from the job and confidently leave it to those you have empowered (as Jesus did prior to His ascension). Second, when your people rejoice in what *we* have accomplished. Third, when those you have taught begin to teach others.

Moses taught Joshua to take over and he died in peace. Jesus taught twelve to take over and He left to return to the Father. You, also, must plan your exit; whether it is attending a conference, leaving on vacation, taking retirement or death. If you cannot turn off your cell phone, you have not reached this point.

The first test of your ability to accomplish this first goal will be in your ability to take time off, to leave town for schooling or vacation. If you are able to leave town without anxiety or *checking in* every day, it will be because you have learned to trust those you have empowered. I become amused with Christian leaders at conventions and seminars that are constantly being pulled away by phone calls or hurrying to a quiet place to call their office to see if all is going well. I wonder, "Who have they trained to handle the emergencies? Where are their associates, their empowered leaders?"

An in-depth study of leadership history produced what is called "The L-Principle." It "concludes that only rarely is a powerful and charismatic leader succeeded by another of comparable stature" (Ford, *Transforming Leadership*, 275). Drawing on the Indian proverb, "Nothing grows under the giant banyan tree," the study concluded that "Powerful leaders often will not let the light filter through to nurture seedlings and will cut off challenging colleagues who may arise as rivals" (Ford, 275). You will do well to learn from Jesus' success and this leadership study. Teach others who can take over in your absence. Leadership is proven when people hardly realize your absence.

Regardless of the size of your organization, you can find several areas in which you will become the visionary and trainer. However, you do not have to be *the one in charge*. Paul left leaders behind in the church to go on to appoint others in other cities. He made a practice to return to check on them, to correspond with them, but he never smothered them with control. His role was that of an encouraging father (1 Th 2:11-12).

The very nature of the leader's role is to plan to make an exit. The most successful mission works have been those where locals were trained to lead after the missionary returned home. DePree believes that the art of leadership is to "liberate people to do what is required of them in the most effective and humane way possible" (DePree, *Leadership Is an Art*, 1). Like Moses, Jesus and Paul, prepare people to survive your departure.

Although a player-coach is involved in the game, he sees the wisdom of taking himself out for rest, to get a better overview of the situation and for personal retraining. While doing so, he trusts those who will fill his position. The man or woman who can never leave the game will soon be burned out. Then they will sit in the bleachers criticizing the game plan of other coaches.

Another leadership study, based solely upon churches, makes this conclusion:

> In the growing churches I studied, the brief absence of the senior pastor actually *strengthened* the church by making the rest of the team work together as a unit. It enabled them to experience the joy of knowing that the church was not a one-man show, a collection of capable individuals whose abilities were smothered by the leader (Barna, *User-Friendly Churches,* 156)

"We Did It!"

One of my favorite experiences as a leader is to hear a person present an idea I have given them as if it were their own. Of equal joy is the observance of a completed project for which people took ownership. The second goal of the ministry of empowerment is to get the people to be able to say, "We did it." This is the simplest test of leadership effectiveness. Lao Tze, an ancient Chinese philosopher, said,

Fail to honor people.
They fail to honor you.
But of a good leader, who talks little.
When his work is done, his aim fulfilled.
They will all say, "We did this ourselves"
(quoted in Bennis & Nanis, *Leaders*, 152).

From this point, the cycle must continue. As Paul told Timothy, "Pass on what I have taught you to faithful men who will teach others" (2 Tim 2:2 author's paraphrase). The job of empowerment is never completed, but always rejoices in seeing newly empowered servants experiencing the joy of a job well done.

Conclusion

There is no greater reward to be found than to see people come to accept Jesus Christ as Lord and then watch them mature. There is true joy in seeing people grow to fulfill that which God created them to be. Satisfaction then comes by watching what God accomplishes through the new believer and know you had a small part in that divine plan.

Chapter Eleven
Understanding Leaders

Introduction

What we discovered in a weekend leadership retreat became a blessing for a church I served, as well as for the two women involved. At the retreat we talked a lot about finding your unique profile as a leader. The result we discovered, to be shared later in chapter twelve, revolutionized two ministries within our congregation.

Each worker in an organization brings with them their heritage and personality. These merge to create a *style* of leadership. Several components are included to create a leadership style. The more you can get to know your people and relate to them on the basis of who they are, the stronger your leadership will be. Leaders understand the diversity of people's gifts, talents and skills. Understanding and accepting diversity enables you to see that each person is needed.

This chapter introduces a Leadership Profile which will help you gain an understanding of each person. The first few areas on the Leadership Profile are very common and it is easy to gain the required information – I will say more about them in the next chapter.

The goal of filling out the information is to understand the life-story and agenda of each leader. Carefully work through the Leadership Profile and use it at every opportunity in working with an individual. Then, use it during prayer times to pray specifically for each person.

LEADERSHIP PROFILE	
Name: Street: City Phone	Spouse: Children:
Employment: Occupation: Phone:	Membership Date: Organizational Experience:

Spiritual Gifts	Talents
1. 2. 3.	1. 2. 3.

Leadership Traits	Ministry Involvement
1. 2. 3.	1. 2. 3.

Spiritual Passion

If I were allowed to complete only one task for my Lord knowing I would not fail, I would . . .

Goals for our Relationship

1.
2.
3.

Contact Dates

1.   3.
2.   4.

Diversity reigns anywhere two or more people gather together, especially for leadership. The purpose of this chapter and the next is to provide tools and understanding to discover the giftedness of each leader. These chapters will assist you to know your people well and to accept them for who they are – to help find the beauty of what God has designed in each person.

Spiritual Gifts

The presence of a variety of gifts is a very clear teaching of scripture. Paul described the Church as a body with many parts (Ro 12:4-8 and 1 Co 12:12-31). God's Church is a living organism with every person designed to share the gifts God has given.

The Apostle Paul is very careful to explain that no one part is more important than another. Spiritual gifts are sovereignly dispensed by God (1 Pe 4:10). The Spirit divides the list of gifts "to every man as He wills" (1 Co 12:11 author's paraphrase). Paul explains that God sets the members in the body "just as He want[s] them to be" (1 Co 12:18). Therefore, we come to know these three facts: (1) Each believer has a gift, a special ability from God. (2) Abilities and how they can be used differ from person to person. (3) The gifts are to be used in service to the others. By helping each person discover their gifts, leaders help each "part" fulfill its designed function.

There are many resources in print and on the Internet that can help people discover their spiritual gifts. Find one that works within your theological framework. The numbers and definitions of individual gifts are not important for our study. What is important is to find a way to evaluate each person to discover his/her *gift-mix*. Few people have only one gift. Most people have a combination – a *mix* – that results in a specialized ability for serving others. For instance, a person with the gifts of *mercy* and *service* might be an excellent worker with widows and orphans. A person with the gifts of *mercy* and *leadership* might not be as good at one-on-one connections with widows and orphans, but could be a good overseer of such a ministry. A person with a gift-mix of *mercy* and *giving* might be a person to whom God gives the ability to support or raise support to care for widows and orphans. All three of these are legitimate, needed ministries.

The discovery of gifts will be a twofold help to you and your leadership. First, it will help you gain an added dimension in the understanding of an individual and in helping that person find effective service. Second, it will help that individual find satisfaction in ministry. You will frequently find people in teaching or leading positions who are unhappy or ineffective. Many times this can be the result of being unaware of their *gift-mix*, a primary cause of discouragement and burn out.

The morning worship service is not the most conducive place to help people find their gift-mix. This is better accomplished in a retreat setting or in small groups. People need to be in comfortable surroundings where there can be interaction with other believers who know them. Following well prepared lessons, the confirmation by people we know and trust is more important than any testing.

Keeping a record of each person's gift-mix will give you insight into ways to assist them. On their "Leadership Profile" list their three strongest gifts. Get to know them more intimately as an individual designed by God. Get to know their story.

Leadership Style

Every Person Is Unique

Gifts Inventories and *Personality Profiles* are good tools to help you know the *gift-mix* of your leadership. However, in my experience, most organizations that have used them allow the results to sit idle and are seldom referenced. A good leader gets to know and understand the uniqueness of each person on the leadership team and to continually look for potential in others outside the current team.

Gifts and *personality* join to create the types of leadership *styles* God has brought together in your organization. Not only are we unique in our spiritual gifts, we are unique in our personality traits as well. These *traits* become the basis of our *leadership style*, the way we use our gift-mix. Understanding the combination of both *style* and *gifts* will help build a strong leadership team.

The basic differences in personalities were first dis-covered 400 years before Christ by Hippocrates, the Father of Medicine. He concluded there are four types of tempera-ments (he called them *the four humors*).

[Hippocrates] erroneously thought that these four temperament types were the result of the four body liquids that predominated in the human body: "blood," "yellow bile," "black bile" and "phlegm." Hippocrates gave name to the temperaments that were suggested by the liquids he thought were the cause: the Choleric - blood, Sanguine - yellow bile, Melancholy - black bile, and Phlegmatic - phlegm. To him these suggested the lively, active, black, and slow temperaments (LaHaye, *Spirit-Controlled Temperament*, 10).

Through the course of time, many people have studied the temperament traits and several new names and descriptions have risen. However, all find their basis in the studies begun by Hippocrates 2500 years ago.

The individual's temperament is a combination of heritage and environment; but mostly of inborn traits that were designed by God (Ps 139:13-16). These characteristics subconsciously affect our behavior. One study describes people as "different from each other, and that no amount of getting after them is going to change them. Nor is there any reason to change them, because the differences are probably good, not bad" (Keirsey & Bates, *Please Understand Me*, 2).

The four temperaments discovered by Hippocrates are basic temperaments and no person is a single-temperament type. For this reason, most profiles have sixteen basic traits they identify and teach the differences within the multiple combinations. Add to this a possible list of more than twenty spiritual gifts, and each person becomes a unique part in God's plan. Our temperament and gifts place a signature or thumbprint on each of one of us making us recognizably distinctive. We are indeed "fearfully and wonderfully made" (Ps 139:14).

Styles Defined

Understanding the four basic temperaments and seeing how each thinks in leadership situations will increase a leader's ability to work with individuals. In seminars that my wife and I have led, we have chosen to rename Hippocrates' original four categories: *Doer, Influencer, Relator*, and *Thinker* (Cook and Hendricks, *Leading the Way)*.

Doers

Ray was an elder in one church where I served. He was as fine a man as you would want to meet. He had a huge heart for the church, but often showed an impatience to see change happening. If there was a job to be done, he wanted to do it. If there was a speech to be given, he would jump to the front. The only problem was, sometimes in his hurry, he forgot about the needs and feelings of people. A classic example of his personality was heard one evening when he was pushing for a great new project within the church. I stopped him and said, "I think we would do well to think about how this would impact the lives of some of our people." His response was, "If you would only stop worrying about people, we could get more done around here." The words no sooner left his lips when he realized the error in what he had said. However, his reaction is typical of a *Doer*.

Doers are dominant leaders who easily take control of situations and bring about action even if they have to bring it about themselves. The key word for Doers is *control*. They have to be in charge so the best results (according to their understanding) will be realized. The Doers' personality "has strong leadership tendencies. . . . [They] not only will readily accept leadership when it is placed on [them], but they will often be the first to volunteer for it. [They are] typically known as the *take-over [people]*" (LaHaye, *Spirit-Controlled Temperament*, 26).

Doers are motivated by results; therefore, they work hard at getting the task completed. Because they are known as busy people who can get results, they are not known for their ability to build relationships. Doers pride themselves in "boldness, bravery, endurance, cleverness, adaption and timing" (Keirsey and Bates, *Please Understand Me!*, 131). However, their people-skills tend to suffer.

Doers are at their best solving problems and unsnarling messes, responding to crisis situations. They thrive on activity; however, it is seldom *aimless* activity. If you want to challenge a Doer, approach them with "a problem to be solved," a project that "only you can do."

Doers have a tendency to ignore the feelings and rights of others in an effort to achieve the goal. They are natural leaders, but they have a tendency to become authoritarian. They are quick to act and impatient with those who do not move with them. Their strength is goal-orientation, strong organization, ability to see the whole situation, and the ability to delegate responsibility to others (however, they will stay right on top that person until the task is complete). "As a leader, more than any other, this type will know what is going on in an organization, for he has acute powers of observation regarding the environment"(Keirsey and Bates, *Please Understand Me!*, 127).

Doers are self-disciplined individuals with a strong tendency towards self-determination. Therefore, they must have the freedom to act and obtain the results. As a consequence, Doers need people on the team who will willingly follow their leadership with little question or resistance, but who will also represent the needs and feelings of people.

Ministries that slow to a maintenance mind set, those that have stopped growing and who do not seem to care, often lose their Doer-type leaders because of the lack of action. Doers will try to get the organization moving. If they are thwarted, they will move on to where the action is.

The weaknesses in Doers, as in all other leadership styles, are best understood when we see deficiencies as the opposite of strengths. A *weakness* should be understood as *strength* pushed to *extreme* (Cook and Hendricks, *Leading the Way*, 14). In other words, the weakness exists because of the strength. If you push too hard to correct a natural weakness you will risk diminishing a natural strength. Only when we are balanced by the Holy Spirit of God are we making the best of both strengths and weaknesses.

One of the most successful sports coaches in America was asked the secret to his winning record. He replied, "Most coaches design practice to work on weaknesses within the team; I design practices to maximize individual and team strengths." A successful Christian businessman gives the same caution, "In developing somebody, the odds of improving existing strengths far outweigh the odds of improving weaknesses. An individual can improve his weaknesses, but it's rarely done from the outside" (Smith, *Learning to Lead*, 110).

Influencers

Travis was a salesman. First he sold cars and then he sold insurance. He was a man who made his living by talking and influencing people to buy his product. He was a fun person to be around because he was able to find humor in any situation. He loved to work with youth because of their energy and they looked to him for counsel. In church leadership meetings he always had good ideas and kept discussion flowing. However, sometimes he would get impatient with other leaders who, in his opinion, spent too much time on details.

The second leadership style gets its name from a word we have used to describe one of the three leadership responsibilities. If there is any personality that should be a natural leader, it would be those individuals who have the natural ability to *influence* people to follow.

> The [Influencers] are the warm, buoyant, lively and 'enjoying' temperament. [They have] an unusual capacity to enjoy [themselves]. They simply enjoy people, [they] do not like solitude, but [are] at [their] best surrounded by friends where [they are] the life of the party. [They are] never at a loss for words. [They] often speak before thinking, but [their] open sincerity has a disarming effect on many of [their] listeners, causing them to respond to [their] mood (LaHaye, *Spirit-Controlled Temperament*, 13).

With the key word of *fun*, Influencers sound like wonderful people to have at the head of an organization. However, they are not without their problems. Being positive by nature, they are easily discouraged when met with negatives. Influencers do not handle controversy or crisis well because most of their decisions are based upon emotion rather than fact.

The strength of Influencers is their verbal skills. They have a natural ability to speak and write fluently. They are at their best when they are with people. In fact, their greatest fear is to be left alone.

Influencers' ability to empathize with people makes them a catalyst for understanding and action. They have the capability to draw out the best in people. Unlike Doers, Influencers do not concentrate on the task. Rather, they focus on the people responsible for the task. Their optimistic energy helps them recruit people to do the job. However, they need to rely on these people because they get so involved they soon find themselves overcommitted and forgetful. As a result, they become known as a great starter, but poor finishers. One influencer, using his natural gift for humor, told me, "My wife says that I am a poor finisher. I don't understand how she could say that. I have never completed anything; so how does she know if it would be *good* or *poor*?"

Be careful, however, not to stymie the Influencer's freedom. Too many rules will cause frustration and loss of creativity. Their optimism causes them to focus on the strengths in other people. This makes them a natural coach. In fact, according to studies, they are happiest when they have an opportunity to teach and direct (Cook and Hendricks, *Leading the Way*, 28). Here, perhaps, is the core of mentors for future leadership development.

Relators

Bill had been on the church's leadership team longer than any other person. Over the years other leaders had left the church during times of conflict and change, but Bill and his family stayed through the good years and the bad. He was loved by everyone and others often sought his counsel. He was quiet, but when he spoke he always had something very good to contribute. Many times the other team members wanted to know what Bill was thinking before they moved on in a discussion. However, he was never in a hurry to make a decision and always wanted to make sure everyone had a chance to share their thinking.

Into the storms and excitement caused by Doers and Influencers come the Relators with their cool, calm way of handling people and problems. They seldom get excited, especially in a crisis. They are "slow, easy-going, well-balanced. Life for them is a happy, unexcited, pleasant experience in which he/she avoids as much involvement as possible (LaHaye, *Spirit-Controlled Temperament*, 21)."

The key word for the Relator is *Relationships*. They are kind-hearted and sympathetic, and will seldom tell you their true feelings because they do not want you to be upset.

> [Their] abilities lie in establishing policies, rules, schedules, routines, regulations, and hierarchy. [They are] good at drawing up lines

174

of communication, and following through. [They are] patient, thorough, steady, reliable, and orderly. [They value] policies, contracts, and standard operating procedures (Keirsey and Bates, *Please Understand Me!,* 138).

Relators lead by establishing rapport with those around them and getting others to follow because they are leaders who care. This, coupled with stability, becomes their strong suit in influencing people. With a strong sense of loyalty, they have always been there, always shown strength, and always listened. Therefore, people follow them. However, because of their focus upon relationships, their greatest fear is conflict. Like Influencers, they do not respond well when confrontation is needed.

Relators have a hunger to serve. They "must be a giver, not the receiver; the caretaker, not the cared for" (Keirsey and Bates, *Please Understand Me!,* 40). For this reason, they are very dependable. These strengths do, however, produce opposite weaknesses. The Relator is plagued by conformity and resistance to change. They can become overly locked into tradition.

Change comes best when Relators can plan their work and follow through on the plan. They like to get assignments clearly settled in their mind before starting. Therefore, they are considered *slow starters*. As a leader, never *drop* an idea or responsibility on a Relator at the last minute. They tend to resist anything that must be done quickly. Seldom do they deny a request for service because saying *no* might damage the relationship.

Relators are excellent administrators, seeing needs and delegating responsibilities to those who can fulfill those needs. Their greatest strength is working in a team. However, because of their steady traditional thinking, they are not initiators. They have trouble starting and getting other people started. If they are to be the leader of a team, they need to have a Doer or Influencer working with them to fill this gap. However, they are much more likely to *finish* a project than the Doer or Influencer.

Thinkers

Twice in our years of working together, Ken came to me and said he needed to resign from the leadership team. Both times I asked him to share what he was feeling. Like other *Thinkers* I have worked with, he said, "I seem to always be the person who is against everything. I think I am holding the church back." I sat with Ken and assured him how much we needed a person like him on our team who thought through the small details, who asked the hard questions that make us evaluate important decisions on more than emotions." Fortunately, he stayed on the team.

Ken cared deeply about the church and I learned that if I had a new idea to share with the team that I could take it to Ken for evaluation. He would listen carefully and tell me what I needed to think through and how different groups within the congregation would handle this new thinking. When I sought his counsel, I was able to make a stronger, clearer presentation to the leadership team.

Thinkers are sensitive, but focused on facts. They desire to be a part of a team, but everything has to be done properly. They can be pessimistic but, at the same time, concerned that their thinking is stopping progress. The key word for Thinkers is "perfection!" They are totally attuned to the process and the results of the project. Their *people skills* are not strong. Thinkers are normally considered *quiet*. However, a motivation to be right and a demand for quality in every task can cause conflict within themselves, as well as with other team members. To them life is a task, and therefore, they become very self-critical, always trying to improve.

Details are the Thinker's forte. People who work with a strong Thinker will be very aware of their pessimism, criticism and inflexibility and often refer to them as negative. This is a tragedy because they are so gifted and a needed part of any team. They bring a strong analytical mind, idealism, and a unique ability in diplomacy. They provide realism to the *big ideas* of the Doers and Influencers. They can always be depended upon to finish their job in the prescribed time.

Thinkers will influence people by having ideas and programs well mapped out before their presentation. People will be swayed by the facts they are able to present and the clear progression of their ideas. Thinkers "usually enjoy developing models, exploring ideas, and building systems" (Keirsey and Bates, *Please Understand Me!*, 54).

Much like the Relator, the Thinker is locked strongly into tradition. Their greatest fear is change (Cook and Hendricks, *Leading the Way*, 29). In order for any change to take place, they must be given reasons, facts, and time to think them through. Because of their desire for perfection, if

177

they are taught proper leadership principles, Thinkers will become *perfect leaders.*

Conclusion

"I have every member of the class analyzed." This startling announcement was made by one of my students on the second day of class. As it turned out, he had sent an email to each class member describing their strengths, weaknesses and how they should be spiritually handled. He was familiar with Gift Inventories and Personality Profiles; however, he was wrong – not only in his evaluation, but his ethics in using his knowledge. It caused an immediate negative reaction among his fellow students from which he never recovered during the term.

Many people dislike the use of Spiritual Gift analyses and personality inventories because they can cause stereo-types. There is a temptation to "size up" each person you meet. Understand that there are other variables in every person's story that affect their ability to lead. These variables depend on a person's childhood environment, current stress levels, and theological understandings. No one is forever locked into a profile as these variables can change.

If you recognize the potential pitfalls, Personality Profiles can give you a good picture of the people on your leadership team and they help you to be a better prepared leader, encourager, and prayer partner. This understanding will also help you to coach people into ministries fit for their interests and abilities, thus preventing frustration, burnout, and poor performance. People will respond to your under-standing of them.

"Obviously, a leader's temperament will differ from one personality to the next. Whatever leadership style may come across, those who respond with cooperation and commitment do so because of the inspiring influence that the leader emits" (Swindoll, *Leadership*, 21).

The bottom line is "we all need each other." God designed us in our mother's womb and knit us in such a way that we would be special in His plan (Ps 139:13). The more we attempt to understand each other and accept our differences, the stronger our leadership will become. George and Logan conclude,

"If we will help people focus on their area of giftedness, spiritual and personal style, two things will happen. First, people will enjoy their ministry; they will have more fun as they serve. Second, they will become effective" (George and Logan, *Leading and Managing*, 30).

Chapter Twelve
Situational Leadership

Matching People and Situations

Your ability to lead effectively will be directly related to the time and effort you invest in getting to know the people you lead. Therefore, in this chapter we are continuing to fill out the Leadership Profile for each person in your leadership sphere. By this time you have spent time with them in small groups, or in one-on-one settings. You have been involved with them in meetings as well as other leadership and decision-making settings. Using the information you have gathered through conversation, observations, and testing you will begin to be able to complete each Leadership Profile.

I strongly urge you to gather the information needed for the Leadership Profile (see page 164) through personal interaction. Do not go to a file or another person to gather your facts. For example, it would be possible for you to go to organizational membership files to find information. This, however, would not be as effective as your allowing a person to share their story of how they came to Christ and/or this ministry. There are also many sources for finding the names of their children. None, however, are as effective as you allowing a parent to tell you about their family.

I want to recommend a second book for your use at this point. Ken Blanchard and Phil Hodges are excellent Christian leaders, recognized in both Christian and secular venues. Their books are short and easy to read. None is better than *The Servant Leader*.[4] I will share an overview of what he has written, but I strongly encourage you read Blanchard and Hodges' short book.

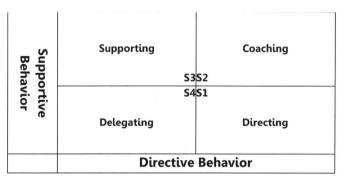

The Variables of the Situation

    Situational Leadership is a measuring scale (see chart above) used by leaders to discover a person's ability and willingness to perform an assigned task. The evaluations can be used for an individual or a group and will take you through *diagnosis, flexibility and partnering for performance* (Blanchard & Hodges, *Servant Leader*, 69). Think about the *commitment* and *competence* levels of the individual rather than policies and demands of the situation. Jesus was a *situational leader*.

At first he directed his disciples to listen and watch what he did. Then he put them in some situations – like the storm on the sea – where they were clearly beyond themselves. At that point he became a coach, offering continued direction and support. Later he sent them out to teach, preach and heal as his representatives. They went out somewhat timidly, but came back with great joy when they saw powerful results. Finally, after months of development – and of success and failure – he prepared to go away and to delegate the ongoing task to them (Ford, *Transforming Leadership*, 286).

The leadership question here is, "Do you expect people to adapt to you, or are you willing to adapt your leadership to their *Development Level?"* Your answer to this question will have a great bearing your ability to realize the vision.

Every situation has several variables with which you will need to contend. There are the people involved – each bringing his/her giftedness, preparation, and agenda. The specific purpose of the organization, committee, or task force casts a flavor. Add to these job descriptions, outside expectations, and deadlines. All are different. There is no single formula to apply to every person or situation. Learn to be flexible and look for the proper clues that will help you to lead a person in a given situation.

Effective leaders adapt themselves to the Development Level of the person/people being led. They choose an appropriate leadership style that will assist a person in the given situation. The leader's personality style of leadership was discussed in chapter eleven. However, here we are talking about how a leader is willing to adjust their style to meet the needs of a team member.

Development Levels

Situational leaders choose a style of leadership based upon their perception of the *Development* of an individual or group, or, their *readiness* to fulfill the responsibility. Development is evaluated as you observe both the person's *commitment* – their *willingness* – to do the task as well as their *competence* – their *ability* – *to* accomplish the assignment.

Some people will need to have every aspect of the task carefully explained. This includes, what to do, how to do it, when to do it, where to do it, and with whom to do it. To others you will simply need to state your vision, give them direction and let them function. Some will be very committed to the vision, but not know what to do. Others are very competent, but have not developed an ownership of the vision. A combination of the two factors creates a matrix showing what you as a leader can do to lead. Failure to know the difference can cause much misunderstanding and/or conflict.

Once you have determined *competence* and *commitment*, you will be able to determine your leadership relationship to that person. Blanchard and Hodges suggest four leadership styles to assist you in helping this person/group be successful:

1. Directing

Situation One/Readiness Level One (bottom right quadrant in the Situational Leadership matrix on page 182) does not often appear in a volunteer organization, which describes most Christian ministries. It applies to a person who has neither commitment nor competence for the given situation. For example, a hired laborer who is only interested in the pay he will receive. He has a low skill level but has a commitment to the purpose for which he has been hired. However, it could describe a new church member who wants to serve; but, they have little confidence in their own ability. They have been given a task but no training. If you do encounter such a person, the best leadership style is directing – carefully provide the what, when, why, where and how with accountability. Rather than becoming dictatorial, this should translate into giving constant guidance, structure, encouragement, and training until they move into Situation Two.

2. Coaching

The Coaching style is used in Situation Two/Readiness Level Two (the upper right quadrant of the matrix) where the individual or group with whom you are working has a low commitment level; but, they have some competence – skills.

The term coaching is used because you will not only provide the guidance, but also the opportunity for dialogue and clarification in order to help the person achieve success. It is a relationship that is strong on personal contact and teaching.

3. Supporting

Empowering the *supporting* style for *Situation Three/Development Level Three* (upper left quadrant of the matrix) will help the person (group) who is *competent* – they have the needed skills; but, for some reason they are hesitant – not sure they want to *commit*. This situation normally appears when you are working with people who have either been hurt, burned out, or sense a past failure in a similar task. They could also be a person who is not totally sold on the task. With this person you need only to share encouragement along with some guidance and direction. Try to maintain a high degree of relationship as you work together to perform the task.

4. Delegating

Delegating (Situation Four/Development Level Four – bottom left quadrant of the matrix) requires little direction from the leader. You can assign a task to this individual (or group) because they are both *competent* – able – and *committed* – willing – to complete it. Your relationship in this situation is referred to as *delegating* because "the leader turns over the responsibility for decision making and implementation to followers" (Hersey, *Situational Leader*, 65). With confidence you can assign the responsibility and know it will be accomplished. You will simply need to keep the lines of communication open for discussion on direction.

Development Level Conclusions

Hersey and Blanchard conclude by reaffirming, "The key to effective leadership is to identify the *Development Level* of the individual or group you are attempting to in-

186

fluence" (Hersey & Blanchard, *Organizational Behavior*, 183). By trying to understand *the situation* and bringing the right leadership you will not only accomplish your vision, you will preserve the integrity of your followers. "Effective leaders know how to 'tailor' their styles to specific situations when attempting to influence the behavior of others" (Hersey, *Situational Leader*, 58).

Spiritual Passion

The next section on the "Leadership Profile" is *Spiritual Passion*. This section begins with the question, "If allowed to complete only one task for my Lord, and knowing I could not fail, I would ..." In completing this statement, each person will tell you much about where they desire to be serving.

By the time you get to this section of the profile, you will know about their family, conversion, spiritual gifts, leadership traits, and areas of service. You will even have made a subjective evaluation of what you believe to be their *competence* and *commitment* in each area they serve. The question now to be answered is whether or not they are serving in the ministry for which they really have a heart.

In the previous chapter I promised to share the dramatic results of gaining the knowledge sought in these last two chapters. In a church where I formerly served, there was a woman who did a wonderful job teaching children. Being a gifted teacher, she served well in the children's department for years. However, during a retreat she expressed her spiritual passion was to see college-aged young adults grow in Christ. Our congregation had attempted to start a college-aged ministry, but could never find the right person to lead it. We had never thought of this woman because she seemed happy teaching children. When we discovered her passion, we asked her to take leadership of a new young adult Sunday School class. Not only did the class begin to grow, but the young adults felt they had found someone who cared and to whom they could talk. Such is the result of helping a person fulfill their *spiritual passion*.

In this same retreat we had a woman who was helping each week with the church's finances. She listed a passion for teaching children. When we approached her and asked if she would like to change ministries, she was excited. She had served well doing the financial accounting; however, she excelled when working with children as she was working in a ministry for which she had great passion.

I have often wondered how many times we allow people to get plugged into ministries where they dutifully serve, but continually wished they were somewhere else. Your sensitivity to this area will go a long way toward providing effectiveness in ministry and preventing burnout among the leadership team.

In the chapter on Planning, we mentioned the premise, "Begin with the End in Mind" (Covey, *Seven Habits*, 95-144). In his book, Stephen Covey presents a scenario that I have effectively used in both class and personal settings to help people discover their "Spiritual Passion." I would encourage each leader to complete this assignment before giving it to others.

Your assignment is to visualize yourself attending a funeral. In your mind, begin by walking into the room where the service is held. As you enter you walk past others who have come – you recognize most of them. You are asked to take a seat near the front. As you sit waiting for the funeral to begin, the realization suddenly hits you, "This is my funeral!"

Seated in front of the room are four potential speakers. There is a member of your family, a person with whom you have worked, your neighbor, and a friend from your church. Now, [this author directs], write out what "you would like each of these speakers to say about you and your life" (Covey, *Seven Habits*, 97).

Many wrestle with this assignment because they have never thought through their passions, what they truly want to accomplish before leaving this life. You may have to coax and affirm the person, but the passions are there. These feelings have never been encouraged to surface. For others it will be like water breaking through a dam, longing to express what they feel deep inside.

Think of the strength you could bring to ministry if everyone in your organization was allowed to serve with a passion. Imagine a church of Paul's who could say, "Woe to me if I do not . . ." (1 Corinthians 9:16). If you could just uncover a handful who would work at their passion with the same fervor as he!

Goals

For eighteen years my wife taught preschool children. Before classes began, she visited each child in their home. Then, after the first month of classes, she created a notebook similar to the Leadership Profile I am suggesting (see page 164). With one page for each child she described the home situation and what she had observed. Then she concluded with her goal of what to accomplish in that child's life by the end of the year. After becoming the school's director, her thoughts turned to goals for each teacher and aide.

My wife's book of goals gave me an idea, "Why not do this for each leader in the congregation?" Instead of looking at them as "the opposition to my dreams," establish goals of relationship and training.

By the time you have reached this section on the Leadership Profile, you should know your people very well. Instead of crying out to the Lord because you are the only faithful one, instead of shaking your fist at Him for bringing you to this place of unconverted souls, try establishing goals to meet their needs. Some you will have to lead to the saving knowledge of Jesus. Some you will have to lead to freedom in Christ. For some you will have to provide leadership training. Others simply need encouragement. Others will have to have their eyes gently opened to see possibilities. Others will need to have hope for the future re-established in their lives. Many will simply have to be unleashed to ministry.

Contact Dates

The last section of the Leadership Profile speaks for itself. Leaders who do not meet regularly with their leadership cannot complain about their lack of growth and vision. Leadership is influence and you cannot influence a person from afar.

The contacts to which I refer in this section are not telephone calls and passing in the hallways. I am talking about meeting face to face with a person in as intimate a conversation as that individual will allow. These are conversations that begin with a person's story, family, and history of service. Only then does it move to a discussion of vision and direction.

Conclusion

In these last two chapters I have presented an outline for helping you understand each person who comes under your leadership. Leadership is the same whether you are the leader a large staff or a Committee Chairperson of a small working group within the ministry. The information gathered in this profile, if done properly, will guide you from positional leadership to relational leadership.

This information will not be gathered overnight. The temptation will be to hurry the process. Leadership is a process that takes time and develops as you are given per- mission by the individual to receive his/her information. Once received, you can build the relationship that will help you plan *together* to fulfill a shared mission.

Epilogue

Release Them to Serve

Epilogue
Release Them to Serve

Mission-Oriented Command

For one hundred and fifty years, the German army was one of the strongest armies to march across the face of the earth. Military historians attribute this success to a philosophy of leadership known as *auftragstaktik,* or *mission-oriented command* (Silva, *"Auftragstaktik,"* 6). The core of this philosophy is "decentralized leadership and command. It allows for decisions and action at the lowest level of command where there is an intimate knowledge of the situation and the commander's intention"(Silva, 6).

According to the German strategist, this was the opposite of *befehlstaktik* or "order-oriented command" (Czeslik, *"Auftragstaktik,"* 10) where no decision or action could ensue without approval of the commander. The German army believed there was great power and diversity when the leaders had a full understanding of the mission and its importance. Then, based on that knowledge, leaders were empowered to make decisions in the midst of the mission. It was a philosophy based on trust, and the fact that "almost every man in a battle could contribute more than just his physical prowess" (Czeslik). The key was mutual trust between officers and their men. The German army lost its strength when leaders began to fear the loss of control and required all decisions to pass through the hierarchy of rank.

Jesus, the greatest leader known to mankind, developed the concept of *mission-oriented command* long before it was conceived by the German armies. Jesus thoroughly trained His disciples, explained to them the Kingdom of God, and then sent them out empowered to do the work. (Mark 6:7-13, Luke 9:1-6). I am confident, from my knowledge of Jesus' leadership style, that He anxiously awaited to hear the reports as they returned excited about their accomplishments.

Prior to sending His disciples on their mission journey, Jesus taught "The Parable of the Sower" (Mark 4:1-20) in which He explained how the spreading of the Word of God affects people differently. Following that, He gave a vision of the growth of the Kingdom of God as a mustard seed (Mark 4:26-34). He demonstrated the power He was going to give to them by calming a storm (Mark 4:35-41), healing a demon-possessed man (Mark 5:1-20), raising a girl from the dead, and healing a woman with a hemorrhage (Mark 5:21-42). Through teaching and demonstration the disciples were prepared and then released to serve.

Jesus once again demonstrates the releasing of empowered workers in Luke 10:1-17. After further teaching and recruitment, He sent out seventy-two empowered servants. In both instances of release, Jesus fully trusted those in whom He had planted the vision of the Kingdom.

The Apostle Paul followed Jesus' leadership example. Having trained young evangelists, he released them to lead in important ministries. To Timothy he wrote, "As I urged you when I went into Macedonia, stay there in Ephesus..." (1 Timothy 1:3). He goes on to re-orient him in just what his mission was to be and its importance. He reminds Titus the

195

reason he was left in Crete -- to "straighten out what was left unfinished and appoint elders in every town" (Titus 1:5).

One of the greatest weaknesses in leadership today is the inability of leaders to practice *mission-oriented command*. There seems to be a great lack of trust to allow people to use their gifts, follow their passion, and begin new and vital ministries within the organization. The malignancy of *control* has infused itself in the thinking of leaders convincing them that no one else can be trusted. Board members feel they have to control leaders, and, as a leader, you will have to fight the misbelief that nothing can work without you, or that no one can have more success than you.

In a study of what makes churches *grow*, the author reveals,

> I found that the leaders of the growing churches delegated responsibility without anxiety. It seemed that those pastors perceived delegation as a means to an end: it was a way to empower other people to do ministry. At the same time, it provided the senior pastor the freedom to concentrate on the areas of giftedness which probably allowed him to rise to the position of senior pastor in the first place.

> In contrast, pastors of stagnant churches often reject the impulse to delegate, largely because they fear it may diminish their own significance in the church, or that the people to whom the responsibility is delegated might

fail. In either case, the result is stunted ministry (Barna, *User-Friendly Church*, 144-145).

In following the prescribed strategy, you have come to know your present and potential leaders personally. You have spent much time with them in their homes, in meetings, in worship, at meals, and in other informal gatherings. You have built together a picture of your community and ministry. You have written a mission statement and set your values. They have written a scenario that sets forth the vision of the future. As you have opportunity, you have taught and encouraged leadership development, empowering people for service. Now you come to perhaps the most critical decision you will make as a leader. "Will you allow these people to fail?" And, if they do, will you be willing to pick them up and help them do it again until they experience success?

But No One Will Lead!

All around the world I have heard leaders say, "But no one wants to get involved!" They say, "I have tried to recruit workers for various responsibilities, but no one is willing." This is an age old problem that can only be solved by a strong leader who constantly casts a vision of possibility and invests time in building relationships.

If no one is stepping forward to accept leadership responsibility, you have at least two possibilities. First, you might be leading in a culture where *release* is a new concept and has not been encouraged or allowed in the past. In that case, you will have to work to convince the people that it is now okay. Second, you might have to back up to the vision portion of this strategy to make sure you have established God's agenda and you have led in a way that created ownership.

DePree believes that leadership is "liberating people to do what is required of them in the most effective and humane way possible" (DePree, *Leadership Is an Art*, 1). Another author says the way to do this is to so convince the potential leader that s/he believes that what you are asking them to do is the most important service within the organization (Kinlaw, *Coaching for Commitment*, 6).

The story is told of two men were employed as masons to help construct a new cathedral. A man watched them as they placed brick after brick in the wall. "What are you doing?" the man asked. The first brick layer answered, "I am putting one brick after another all day long." The second worker replied, "I am building a beautiful cathedral." The first man had a job; the second man had a vision. Someone had helped him to see the importance and potential beauty of every brick. That is our responsibility as leaders, to get everyone to see how important their assignment is to the whole picture.

There are two principles you will quickly experience as a leader. First, most people will not give money to retire operational indebtedness, but they will give to an exciting vision of the future. Second, people will not find satisfaction in serving to fill a position, but they will find purpose if they see how what they are doing fits into the success of the vision. Once people are sold on a vision of the future, their passion for the success of that dream will see them through the most difficult of situations. Most people do not step up to service because they do not know you and they are not convinced how the vision will make any difference.

A Personal Word

A real need you have for success will be to find someone who is there for you. We need people with whom we can share, laugh, cry, and pray. I always tried to foster a team relationship with the congregation's lay leaders, to develop their confidence in me as a person and a leader. In most situations, integrity will carry you through and build that relationship of confidence. I have had some close friendships with people within the churches I have served. I am not an advocate of the school which teaches no friendship within the local church. These friends are precious and have proved to be lasting over the years. Nevertheless, there was never an openness to discuss my feelings on *sticky situations*. There were subjects that always seemed off limits.

A leader needs, therefore, to go beyond their organization to find a person or group of peers with whom they can meet, who will hold them accountable in integrity and support. I would caution you, however, to pick these confidants with great care. A negative person, or a person who does not understand the call and needs of ministry, may feed your frustrations and cause you to give up when God is allowing the difficult time to mature you. A friend of mine had an accountability partner who was not a Christian. By sharing problems, the partner was convinced that Christianity was not an option for him, and he continually counseled my friend to quit.

Beware also of those who are cynical. While I was in seminary, most of my fellow church leadership students held ministries in smaller churches throughout rural Illinois. We would drive to school for two days of classes each week. During our lunch hours there was a group who met in the school lounge. As lunch began a makeshift sign was placed on the table reading, "Scorner's Corner." We would mock, harangue, and ridicule the people in the churches where we served. Even though my situation was a very positive and supportive, I found myself getting caught up in the pessimism. I would return home and began looking for problems similar to those the group scorned. It was not healthy for me, or the people I served, for me to be a part of this group. Therefore, I chose to drop out of the group.

My greatest help came from relationships to church leaders outside my own denomination. Men (ethically you must not allow such a relationship with a member of the opposite sex) who knew ministry and understood its special challenges. Men whose faith would help me sustain and who could be sustained by mine. Finding this individual might be one of the most critical decisions you make to enable your longevity.

Conclusion

As you begin your ministry, you will soon find that leadership in an organization made up of volunteers can be, at the same time, the most rewarding and frustrating experience of a lifetime. The statistics are not encouraging concerning those who stay in the ministry past seven years. My purpose in writing this book is to help improve those statistics and bring the joy to the ministry that Paul described to the Philippians and that should be yours today. May the Lord bless you as you strive to become the leader He called you to be. And, may you produce leaders who will produce leaders as God's Kingdom grows throughout the world.

Source List

Source List

Books

Anderson, L. (1990). *Dying For Change*. Minneapolis: Bethany House Publishers.

Anderson, R. (1986). *Minding God's Business*. Grand Rapids: Eerdmans Publishing Co.

Barna, G. (1991). *User Friendly Churches: What Christians Need to Know About the Churches People Love to Go To*. Ventura: Regal Books, Gospel Light Publishing Co.

Barna, G. (1992). *The Power of Vision: How You Can Capture and Apply God's Vision for Your Ministry*. Ventura: Regal Books, Gospel Light Publishing Co.

Barna, G. (1993). *Today's Pastors: A Revealing Look at what Pastors Are Saying about Themselves, Their Peers and the Pressures They Face*. Ventura: Regal Books, Gospel Light Publishing Co.

Bennis, W. (1989). *Why Leaders Can't Lead: The Unconscious Conspiracy Continues*. San Francisco: Jossey-Bass Publishers.

Bennis, W & Nanus, B. (1985). *Leaders: The Strategies for Taking Charge*. Perennial Library. New York: Harper and Row Publishers.

Blanchard, K. and Hodges, P. (2003). *The Servant Leader: Transforming your Heart, Head, Hands and Habits*, Nashville: J. Countryman, div of Thomas Nelson, Inc..

Butt, H. (1973). *The Velvet Covered Brick: Christian Leadership in an Age of Rebellion.* New York: Harper & Row.

Clinton, R. J. (1988). *The Making of a Leader.* Colorado Springs: NavPress.

Cook, B. & Hendricks, H. (1987). *Leading the Way: Practical Training for Effective Christian Leadership.* Atlanta: Church Dynamics, Inc.

Covey, S. R. (1989). *The Seven Habits of Highly Successful People.* New York: Simon and Schuster.

Dale, R. D. (1981). *To Dream Again: How to Help Your Church Come Alive.* Nashville: Broadman Press.

Dale, R. D. (1986). *Pastoral Leadership: A Handbook of Resources for Effective Congregational Leadership.* Nashville: Abingdon Press.

Dale, R. D. (1988). *Keeping the Dream Alive: Understanding and Building Congregational Morale.* Nashville: Broadman Press.

DePree, M. (1989). *Leadership Is An Art.* New York: Doubleday, 1989.

DePree, M. (1992). *Leadership Jazz.* New York: A Currency Book, Doubleday.

Dobbins, G. (1947). *Building Better Churches: A Guide to the Pastoral Ministry*. Nashville: Broadman Press.

Drakeford, J. (1969). *The Awesome Power of the Listening Ear.* Waco: Word Books.

Ellis, J. S. (1988). *The Church On Purpose: Keys to Effective Church Leadership*. Cincinnati: Standard Publishing Co.

Ford, L. (1991). *Transforming Leadership: Jesus' Way of Creating Vision, Shaping Values and Empowering Change.* Downers Grove: InterVarsity Press.

Gardner, J. W. (1990). *On Leadership*. New York: The Free Press, Macmillan, Inc.

George, C. F. & Logan, R. E. (1987). *Leading and Managing Your Church.* Old Tappan: Fleming H. Revell Co.

Getz, G. A. (1974). *The Measure of a Man.* Glendale: Regal Books, Gospel Light Publications.

Getz, G.A. (1974). *Sharpening the Focus of the Church.* Chicago: Moody Press.

Greenleaf, R. K. (1977). *Servant Leadership: A Journey Into the Nature of Legitimate Power and Greatness*. New York: Paulist Press.

Griffin, E. A. (1982). *The Mind Changers: The Art of Christian Persuasion.* Wheaton: Tyndale House Publishers, Inc.

Hagberg, J. O. (1984). *Real Power: Stages of Personal Power in Organizations.* Minneapolis: Winston Press.

Haggai, J. (1986). *Lead On! Leadership That Endures in a Changing World.* Waco: Word Publishing.

Hersey, P. (1984). *The Situational Leader.* New York: Warner Books.

Hersey, P. & Blanchard, K. (1982). *Management of Organizational Behavior: Utilizing Human Resources.* 5th ed. Englewood Cliffs: Prentice-Hall.

Hian, C. W. (1987). *The Making of a Leader: A Guide for Present and Future Leaders.* Downers Grove: InterVarsity Press.

Kanter, R. M. (1983). *The Change Masters: Innovations for Productivity in the American Culture.* New York: Simon and Schuster.

Keirsey, D. & Bates, M. (1984). *Please Understand Me: Character & Temperament Types* (5th ed.). B&D Books.

Kinlaw, D. C. (1989). *Coaching for Commitment: Managerial Strategies for Obtaining Superior Performance.* San Diego: University Associates, Inc.

Kouzes, J. M. & Posner, B. Z. (1989). *The Leadership Challenge: How to Get Extraordinary Things Done in Organizations.* San Francisco: Jossey-Bass Publishers, Inc.

LaHaye, T. (1966). *Spirit-Controlled Temperament*. Wheaton: Tyndale House Publishers.

LePeau, A. T. (1983). *Paths of Leadership*. Downers Grove: InterVarsity.

Lindgren, A. J. (1965). *Foundations for Purposeful Church Administration*. Nashville: Abingdon Press.

Malphurs, A. (1999). *Developing a Vision for Ministry in the 21st Century*, (2nd ed.). Grand Rapids: Baker Books, a Div of Baker Book House Co.

McGavran, D. (1970). *Understanding Church Growth*. Grand Rapids: Wm B. Eerdmans Publishing Co.

McKenna, D. L. (1989). *Power to Follow, Grace to Lead: Strategy for the Future of Christian Leadership*. Dallas: Word Publishing.

Machiavelli. *The Portable Machiavelli*, trans. & ed. Bondanella P. & Musa, M. (1979). "The Prince". New York: Penguin Books, Viking Penguin Inc.

Merrill, D. (1986). *Clergy Couples in Crises: The Impact of Stress on Pastoral Marriages*. "The Leadership Library." Carol Stream: Christianity Today, Inc., Word Books..

Muck, T. (1987). *When to Take a Risk: A Guide to Pastoral Decision Making*. "The Leadership Library," Vol. 9. Carol Stream: Christianity Today, Inc., Word Books.

Myra, H, ed. (1987). *Leaders: Learning Leadership from Some of Christianity's Best*. "The Leadership Library,"

Vol. 12. Carol Stream: Christianity Today, Inc., Word Books.

Oswald, R.M. (ND). *Pastor as Newcomer*. Hearndon: The Alban Institute, www.alban.org/bookdetails.aspx?id=3546. No. OL123 Digital Download.

Oswald, R.M. (1992). *New Beginnings: A Pastorate Start Up Workbook*. New York: An Alban Institute Publication.

Peters, T. (1987). *Thriving on Chaos: Handbook for a Management Revolution.* New York: Alfred A. Knopf.

Peters, T. & Waterman, R. H. (1982). *In Search of Excellence: Lessons from America's Best-Run Companies.* New York: Warner Books.

Rush, M. (1987). *Management: A Biblical Approach.* Wheaton: Victor Books, Scripture Press Publications, Inc.

Sanders, J. O. (1980). *Spiritual Leadership.* Chicago: Moody Press.

Schaller, L. E. (1984). *Looking In The Mirror: Self-Appraisal in the Local Church.* Nashville: Abingdon Press.

Schein, E. H. (1985). *Organizational Culture and Leadership.* San Francisco: Jossey-Bass Publishers, Inc.

Schuller, R. H. (1974). *Your Church Has Real Possibilities!* Glendale: Regal Books, Gospel Light Publications.

Smith, F. (1986). *Learning to Lead: Bringing Out the Best in People*. "The Leadership Library," Vol. 5. Carol Stream: Christianity Today, Inc., Word Books.

Steiner, G. A. (1979). *Strategic Planning: What Every Manager Must Know*. New York: The Free Press, Macmillan Publishing Co., Inc.

Swindoll, C. R. (1985). *Leadership*. Waco: Word Books.

Tozier, A.W. (1982). *The Pursuit of God*. Tozier Legacy Edition. Camp Hill: Christian Publications, Inc.

Trueblood, E. (1967). *The Incendiary Fellowship*. New York: Harper and Row Publishers.

Warren, R. (1995). *The Purpose-Driven Church: Growth Without Compromising Your Message and Mission*. Grand Rapids: Zondervan Publishing House.

Wilkens, A. L. (1989). *Developing Corporate Character: How to Successfully Change an Organization Without Destroying It*. San Francisco: Jossey-Bass Publishers, Inc.

Magazine And Journal Articles

Czeslik, K. Auftragstaktik: Thoughts of a German Officer. *Infantry*. January - February, 1991.

Fullum, T. The View From Above. Interview by Dean Merrill. *Leadership*. Winter, 1984.

Hatfield, M. O. Integrity Under Pressure. Interview. *Leadership*, Spring, 1988.

Johnson, P. The Passion-Driven Church. *Leadership*, Spring, 1992.

Larson, C. B. Gaining Respect the Old Fashioned Way: How to Earn the Congregation's Esteem – and What to Do When You Don't Get It, *Leadership*, Winter, 1988.

Reimann, B. C. & Wiener Y. Corporate Culture: Avoiding the Elitist Trap. *Inside Guide Magazine,* Winter, 1988.

Silva, J. L. Auftragstaktik: Its Origin and Development. *Infantry*, September - October, 1989.

Reference Works

The Holy Bible: New International Verson. (1978). Grand Rapids: Zondervan Bible Publishers.

Webster's New Collegiate Dictionary. (1961). 13th ed. Springfield: C. & C. Merriam Co.

Unpublished Notes

Anderson, R. (1999). The Theology of Change. Class lecture. *Strategic Planning.* Sponsored by the Institute for Christian Organizational Development. Pasadena, CA: Fuller Theological Seminary, February.

Maxwell, J. (1989). *Everything Rises and Falls on*

Leadership. Seminar. Buena Park, CA. Sponsored by Injoy Ministries, El Cajon, CA, February.

Russell, R. (2010). *Introduction to Asset Mapping*. Yangon, Myanmar. Global Youth Ministry Training. Sponsored by YouthHope, Ft Myers, FL, October.

Endnotes

1 This outline of questions is an adaption of the questions asked by Edger Schein in his book, *Organizational Culture and Leadership*. 130-135. In this adaption a careful attempt has been made to follow Schaller's warning to beware of adapting standards from *profit-oriented* business to the work of the Kingdom (Schaller, *Looking in the Mirror*, 54).

2 Similar questions can be designed to discover the culture of a town, village or neighborhood being considered for a new church plant. Each location will have a unique history and culture that must be understood.

3. Dobbins lists the following types of communities in which the church might find itself:
1. Isolated, backward rural
2. Progressive rural
3. The decadent village - overshadowed by nearby towns
4. The growing village - on its way to becoming a town
5. The stagnant town - remaining the same
6. The wide-awake town - business center for the country-side
7. Medium-size city - self-sufficient, expanding, proud
8. Industrial city - most people work in factories
9. Commercial city - most people work in commerce or transportation

10. Residential suburb - "Bedroom communities" - people drive to another city to work
11. Resort city - most people work in tourism or are there

to "play"
12. College community - mixture of school related people and city people with little love for each other (Dobbins, *Building Better Churches*, 156-183).

[4] Blanchard, K. & Hodges, P. (2003). *The Servant Leader: Transforming your Heart, Head, Hands and Habits*, Nashville: J. Countryman, div of Thomas Nelson, Inc.

Made in the USA
San Bernardino, CA
03 April 2015